Janice Galloway's

The Trick is to Keep Breathing

Gillian Sargent

Association for Scottish Literary Studies 2016

Published by
Association for Scottish Literary Studies
Scottish Literature
7 University Gardens
University of Glasgow
Glasgow G12 8QH
www.asls.org.uk

ASLS is a registered charity no. SC006535

First published 2016

Text © Gillian Sargent

A CIP catalogue for this title
is available from the British Library

ISBN 978-1-906841-27-0

CONTENTS

SCOTNOTES

Study guides to major Scottish writers and literary texts

Produced by the Education Committee
of the Association for Scottish Literary Studies

THE ASSOCIATION FOR SCOTTISH LITERARY STUDIES aims to promote the study, teaching and writing of Scottish literature, and to further the study of the languages of Scotland.

To these ends, the ASLS publishes works of Scottish literature; literary criticism and in-depth reviews of Scottish books in *Scottish Literary Review*; short articles, features and news in *ScotLit*; and scholarly studies of language in *Scottish Language*. It also publishes *New Writing Scotland*, an annual anthology of new poetry, drama and short fiction, in Scots, English and Gaelic. ASLS has also prepared a range of teaching materials covering Scottish language and literature for use in schools.

All the above publications are available as a single 'package', in return for an annual subscription. Enquiries should be sent to:

ASLS
Scottish Literature
7 University Gardens
University of Glasgow
Glasgow G12 8QH

Tel/fax +44 (0)141 330 5309
e-mail **office@asls.org.uk**
or visit our website at **www.asls.org.uk**

Acknowledgements

I would like to thank the following people for their assistance throughout the writing process: Ronnie Renton and Lorna Smith, for their generous feedback and meticulous editing; the Education Committee of the ASLS for affording me the opportunity to write the Scotnote; and Duncan Jones for transforming the book into the finished article.

Page References

Page references are to the following editions:
- *The Trick is to Keep Breathing* (London: Vintage, 2016)
- *Blood* (London: Vintage, 1999)
- *Foreign Parts* (London: Vintage, 1995)
- *Where You Find It* (London: Vintage, 1997)
- *Clara* (London: Vintage, 2003)

1. JANICE GALLOWAY: LIFE AND WORK

Janice Galloway was born in 1955 in Buckreddan Maternity Home, Kilwinning, and was brought up in the small south-west coastal resort of Saltcoats. Galloway has written compellingly of her childhood and adolescence in two volumes of autobiography. These 'anti-memoirs' eschew nostalgia to describe with great clarity, honesty and poignancy challenging aspects of Galloway's childhood; the breakdown of her parents' marriage; the modest life carved out for Galloway by her stoic single-parent mother; and a seemingly fraught relationship with her older sister. Despite the heavy subject matter, *This is Not About Me* (2008) does not wallow in miserabilism. Through Galloway's prism, a challenging childhood and seemingly commonplace Scottish primary school education are presented in dazzling technicolour. Galloway's vividly drawn sketches transport the reader to 1950s and 60s Saltcoats, to a time when her younger self tried desperately (and often in vain) to make sense of the chaotic and confusing world around her. *This is Not About Me* culminates with an 'eleven turning twelve'-year-old Galloway preparing to make the transition from primary to secondary school. Part two of Galloway's autobiography, *All Made Up* (2011), takes the reader through Galloway's teenage years and secondary education at Ardrossan Academy, where her interest in the liberal arts was established.

The memoirs leave us to fill in the blanks about Galloway 'the professional'. On leaving Ardrossan, Galloway pursued her interests in Music and English at the University of Glasgow. Although studious and highly able, she was disappointed by university life; at the outset of her Junior Honours year, she decided to take a year out of Higher Education. She found work in a Welfare Rights department, assisting and advising people with claims. She then returned to finish her studies, but opted to graduate with an Ordinary degree. Following a period of unemployment, she enrolled in a teacher training course at Hamilton College of Education and on completion

1

found herself back in Ayrshire for her first teaching post at Garnock Academy in Kilbirnie. She left the field of education in 1989 to concentrate on her writing.

Janice Galloway is one of Scotland's (and indeed Britain's) most accomplished contemporary writers. In the twenty-five years since the publication of her first novel, Galloway has enjoyed both popular and critical success as a writer. In a recent survey undertaken by the readers of *The List* magazine, *The Trick is to Keep Breathing* was voted into the top fifty Scottish Books of All Time. The novel has won several awards, including the MIND/Allen Lane Book of the Year, and was shortlisted for the Whitbread First Novel and Scottish First Book Awards. Since publishing her first novel, Galloway has been prolific, penning two more novels (*Foreign Parts*, 1994, and *Clara*, 2002), two volumes of autobiography (*This is Not About Me*, 2008, and *All Made Up*, 2011), and four collections of short stories (*Blood*, 1991; *Where You Find It*, 1996; *Collected Stories*, 2009; and *Jellyfish*, 2015). She has also been a frequent and generous contributor of her own shorter material to anthologies and collections. Her latest collection of shorter fiction, *Jellyfish* (Freight Books, 2015), deals with the universal concerns of parenthood, madness and relationships.

Galloway is a truly versatile writer. Through collaborative artistic ventures her interests in writing literature and composing music have been brought together. In 2002, Galloway premiered her operatic collaboration with Sally Beamish and Scottish Opera. *Monster* (2002), an interpretation of the life of Mary Shelley, saw Galloway take responsibility for the libretto (the text) and Beamish the musical score. She has also forged a successful partnership with the Orcadian artist Anne Bevan. Together, the women have been responsible for two major artistic ventures. The first, *Pipelines* (2000, the exhibition was originally called *Undercover*), sought to examine the network of underground water pipes which supplied drinking water to Edinburgh in the medieval period. The second, a project entitled *Rosengarten* (2006), examined obstetrical instruments used during childbirth. In the exhibition a collection of sculptural objects by Bevan is framed by

Galloway's wall-mounted text. Elsewhere, Galloway's interest in classical music – and in the works of Clara Wieck Schumann in particular – resulted in a programme of words (written by Galloway) and music (played by pianist Graeme McNaught) at the University of Aberdeen's WORD Festival 2003. She has been writer in residence at four Scottish prisons, has taught at Faber and Faber's 'Academy' and at Stirling University, where she served as visiting professor, and in 2012 was appointed the first Literature Fellow at the University of Otago in New Zealand.

In all of Galloway's work, there is a central concern for the voice of the under-represented or marginalised. Often (although not always) this voice belongs to the female. The majority of this study guide is dedicated to Galloway's seminal work, *The Trick is to Keep Breathing*. In Chapter 7, the remaining major fictional works in Galloway's oeuvre will be addressed briefly in order to acknowledge points of intersection between the three novels and the prose non-fiction texts. A selection of short stories will also be discussed in order to suggest Galloway's mastery of the art of the short story form.

2. THE TRICK IS TO KEEP BREATHING (1989)

Introduction

In the author's own words, *The Trick is to Keep Breathing* is a study of a woman *in extremis* (extreme difficulty). The novel is told through the eyes of a first-person narrator, Joy Stone. When we first meet Joy she is twenty-seven and struggling to come to terms with the death of her lover, Michael, following a swimming-pool accident whilst the couple have been holidaying in Spain. In addition to the grief she feels, Joy is plagued by guilt about the part she played in his death, having started an affair with Michael whilst he was married. The finer details of Michael's tragic accident are slowly revealed through a series of flashbacks and dreams (indicated in the novel by italicised prose). It becomes apparent that Joy is deeply unwell, and has a blatant disregard for her well-being. We are introduced to a series of minor characters who surround Joy – her best friend, Marianne, who lives in America; Marianne's mother, Ellen, who overburdens Joy with kindness and hearty food; Tony, her boss at the bookmakers where she works on a Saturday; Paul, an ex-boyfriend; and David, a younger man with whom she has a 'casual' relationship. Yet, Joy can depend on none of these characters for real assistance. With no-one to help alleviate the burden of grief and guilt she feels, Joy spirals out of control, developing an eating disorder and suffering a breakdown. She is admitted to a psychiatric ward where her state of mind worsens before it begins to get better.

Grief and guilt aside, Joy faces other problems. She has significant financial worries; feels pressure to conform to societal norms and certain gender roles; engages in a number of destructive affairs and relationships; and her mother passed away not long before Michael. The more we learn about the character of Joy, the more we realise that Michael's death has not been the sole cause of Joy's mental ill-health, but has in fact been the catalyst forcing Joy's underlying problems to rise to the surface. Joy's narrative is one of breakdown, extreme despair, and sheer endurance. Galloway has described her protagonist's voice as 'frightened but grimly determined' and by the novel's end this grim determination to survive has facilitated the beginning of Joy's rehabilitation.

Synopsis of the novel

Galloway's experimentation with generic convention and narrative style can make it tricky to work out the linear or chronological order of events that are described. It is perhaps helpful to begin the interrogation of this text with a detailed synopsis of what actually happens.

1. The beginnings of breakdown (pp. 6–72)

Chronologically, the events of the novel begin on Joy's return from Spain following the accident. In the opening sequence Joy is alone in the living room of the rundown house she once shared with Michael. It is late on Wednesday evening, and Joy is putting off going to bed. She knows she has work in the morning and eventually makes the long trip upstairs to what was previously 'their' bedroom. The fifty pages which follow document five days in Joy's life. Beginning on the Thursday morning, the narrative moves through Joy's weekend, and culminates on the Monday morning of the new week. On the surface, nothing all that extraordinary occurs in Joy's life during these five days: she spends much of her time alone at home; she attends work (she is a drama teacher in a secondary school, pp. 11–12); visits Ellen (pp. 33–36); keeps appointments with the health visitor (pp. 19–24) and her GP (pp. 50–54); and works a Saturday shift at a bookmakers to generate additional income (pp. 30–33).

Joy's narration of these seemingly commonplace events reveals a great deal about her current fragile state of mind. Her meeting with the health visitor is a well-rehearsed charade. She is reluctant to listen to her GP who is advising that she be admitted to a local psychiatric hospital. The advances of her boss at the bookmakers make her uneasy. Joy finds a comforting order in familiar routines, as evidenced by her discussion of teaching (p. 12), but the idea of 'daily routine'

takes on new significance when habitual daily procedures
– eating; bathing; sleeping; engaging with others; working –
become ritualistic in nature (p. 10, p. 18, p. 38). In these five
days we see Joy starve herself and self-harm. The intense and
arresting flashbacks to the day of Michael's death compound
Joy's feelings of anguish.

With her mind already in turmoil, Joy receives an unwanted
visitor at the house in the shape of her older sister Myra
(pp. 57–72). Myra is the only family of which Joy can speak.
Joy hints that Myra has been abusive (both physically and
mentally) to her in the past (p. 59). Myra's appearance panics
the narrator, who tries to call on the help of her ex-fiancé Paul
for help (p. 68). Paul admits to having given the address
to Myra, and refuses to help Joy get rid of her. Joy has no
option but to spend the evening drinking with Myra. During
the evening, Myra poses difficult questions about Michael
(pp. 66–67). The sisters part in the morning with issues still
to be resolved (p. 72). Myra's visitation triggers a vivid flashback to Michael's death, specifically to Joy's journey to hospital
trapped in the back of a Spanish ambulance with the body
(pp. 69–70).

2. Joy's deterioration (pp. 72–128)
We learn that Michael and Joy worked together in the same
school (p. 64). The Head Teacher, Mr Peach, holds a memorial
service in Michael's honour. Joy is invited to attend, but
so, too, is Michael's wife, Norma, who duly takes her place in
the front row on the day of the service. Joy is left reeling
by the tone and message of a service in which the minister
extends sympathy only to Michael's wife and immediate family
(pp. 78–79). The minister consciously ignores Joy, effectively
exorcising the memory of Michael's affair with her, and cleans-
ing Michael of his extra-marital 'sin'. She is later reprimanded
by Mr Peach for having written an inappropriate letter to the
minister conveying her anger and disappointment over his
tactless service (pp. 74–75). Following her meeting with Mr
Peach, Joy decides not to go into work the next day. Her

psychological state worsens. Having starved herself for weeks, bulimia now takes hold of Joy.

Tony finally tries to persuade Joy to go on a 'date' with him to the dog track to watch his greyhound race (pp. 92–94). Joy accepts – reluctantly – and makes an effort to look good to satisfy Tony (pp. 97–98). The 'date' begins conventionally with Tony picking her up in the car, and they go through the motions by engaging in small talk whilst listening to music. Joy's narrative ends abruptly at this point with the intrusion of another flashback (p. 99). A somewhat disorientated Joy picks up the narrative the following morning and we learn that Joy has successfully spurned Tony's advances by not inviting him in at the end of the evening. Joy finds three letters waiting downstairs – the first from Marianne, the second from Norma's lawyers, and the third from Foresthouse Psychiatric Ward containing details of Joy's referral (p. 101). The date of the referral is for that day.

Joy's paranoia plagues her first consultation at Foresthouse. For the first time, Joy is asked to tell the doctor – whom she names 'Dr One' – in her own words what she thinks is the matter (p. 103). This catches her off-guard; she speaks openly about her mother's death, her affair with a married man, and Michael's drowning (p. 104). Joy is overcome with emotion. Dr One suggests that she be admitted onto the ward for a brief spell. Although Joy is worried by the prospect of spending weeks on the ward, she knows that she will return on Monday to be admitted. The majority of her friends affirm that she is making the right decision (pp. 109–10).

The first week at Foresthouse is confusing, and Joy spends a lot of time trying to figure out the systems and routines on the ward (pp. 110–29). She speaks with three different healthcare professionals – a nurse and two other doctors, 'Dr Two' and 'Dr Three' – and each in turn asks the same questions. Having opened up to Dr One, she is unhappy to have to go through these motions again. She is frustrated by the lack of consistency in personnel, the repetitive questioning without any solutions, and by the generic approach taken with all patients. Nevertheless, Joy tries hard to integrate into life on the ward and is given a weekend pass to go home at the end of week one. Her resilience has been tested during her week-long admission. She returns to an empty house, vulnerable and frustrated, without having made progress with her rehabilitation (p. 129).

Following her shift at the bookies, Joy receives a visit from David – a former pupil at Cairdwell Secondary (pp. 134–38). She admits to having instigated an affair with David in the days following her mother's death, when she was still in a relationship with Paul. David has come to offer her support. Joy knows that their meetings usually include a lot of alcohol and culminate in sex. This meeting is different as it ends not in sex but with David asking if he can come to visit her in Foresthouse (p. 136). Joy seems disappointed.

3. Joy hits rock bottom (pp. 138–78)

Now aware of the established routines at Foresthouse, Joy makes a smooth transition back onto the ward. Patients on the ward are prescribed drugs for their conditions, and are, ironically, awoken in the morning in order to be given sedatives. Joy begins to keep a diary (p. 140) to record events in case she forgets. The first entry in the diary deals with her consultation with a gynaecologist who asks if she might be pregnant (p. 140). This thought has – apparently – never occurred to her and Joy laughs off the suggestion, but it plays on her mind. Friday's diary entry records details of her ultrasound appointment in the maternity bay (pp. 145–46). Lying waiting for an image to materialise on the screen, Joy begins to contemplate life as a mother. She is left numb (rather than relieved) when the gynaecologist announces that she is not pregnant. Joy's narrative becomes more disjointed after this appointment, and it is clear that her mental health is worsening.

A 'dinner and wine' evening planned for patients stresses Joy (p. 160). She thinks the staff are playing a trick on patients by taking a group including an alcoholic, a schizophrenic, and an anorexic for such an ill-conceived night out. She is also troubled by the fact that she normally enjoys the company of men at such functions (p. 161). Before leaving for the night out, Joy has an upsetting meeting with Dr Three about treatment options (pp. 163–65). Dr Three's responses to her questions are disappointing. The evening gets off to a bad start as Joy is already flustered by her discussion with Dr Three (pp. 165–66). The meal is as awkward as she had anticipated and she drinks heavily to get through the evening. The next day, Dr Two gives Joy a copy of a self-help book called *Courage and Bereavement*. Joy reads the entire book in two hours and is upset by its contents (pp. 171–72). She recognises many of the sentiments contained within this book, but does not yet know how to practically implement the advice imparted by the book's author.

During a weekend visit home, Tony once again asks Joy out on a 'date' to a restaurant (p. 173). She gives in, thinking that she ought to give Tony the benefit of the doubt for trying to be kind. Joy has a sense of foreboding throughout the evening, signalled by the regular intrusion of text in the margin of the page (pp. 174–75). She cannot shift this feeling, but does try to ignore it. The evening ends in a distressing sexual encounter between them. Joy is extremely upset and cries afterwards (pp. 175–76). Tony does not comfort her, but rather leaves her in the house alone. She blames herself for what has just happened and apportions no blame to Tony (p. 176).

Joy is wracked with guilt about the part she has played in Michael's and Tony's adultery (p. 186). She tries to locate a secret stash of pills in her locker only to find that they have been removed. She is sedated by a nurse. As the sedative works its way into her bloodstream, Joy has a moment of lucidity as she begins to realise where she is and why she is there (pp. 187–88).

4. The beginnings of rehabilitation (pp. 189–236)

It is a Friday in December and Joy's twenty-eighth birthday. To suit her newly established routine, Joy is spending the weekend at home (p. 189). This particular weekend the hospital have granted Joy an additional two days at home as a trial. A chance encounter with an old schoolmate in the supermarket makes Joy keenly aware of how much her own physical appearance has altered for the worse (p. 191). She stops by a chemist on the way home and purchases the largest bottle of paracetamol that she can find (pp. 191–92).

During the course of the evening Joy makes her way through a bottle of gin and a lot of memories. She thinks about the unrealistic pressures placed upon women (p. 193), about her attempts to block out her own mother's illness (p. 193), about the night Norma discovered the affair (p. 194), and about the immediate aftermath of Michael's death (p. 196). It becomes clear that Joy has decided to commit suicide by overdosing on a potent concoction of gin and paracetamol (p. 197). As she prepares to take her own life, Joy thinks about whether people might be genetically predisposed to depression; she cites a number of cases in her own maternal lineage as supporting evidence for this assertion (pp. 198–99). Joy finally swallows the pills (p. 201). Just as she is slipping out of consciousness someone knocks on her living room window (p. 202). It is David and Joy realises the identity of her visitor just in time. In her less than lucid state she debates the merits of allowing David in. She is aware that if she does let him in, then it means that she cannot wholeheartedly wish to die. Almost involuntarily, Joy's drugged body moves towards the door (p. 203). She has chosen not to die, and now must live with the consequences of this decision.

This is the turning point for Joy. Firstly, she accepts Ellen's hospitality and spends an evening enjoying the warmth and comfort of Ellen's house (pp. 206–07). Secondly, Joy remains strong in the face of a late-night phone call from Tony during which he attempts to manipulate her into inviting him into her home (pp. 208–09). She coolly dismisses him, much to Tony's annoyance and disbelief. Joy then has a dream about Michael, in which she fantasises that she is walking with Michael at a graveside – presumably his graveside. They do not speak to each other. The fantasy of Michael melts away to nothingness at the end of the dream (p. 210). This dream suggests that Joy is beginning to come to terms with the fact that Michael is dead and cannot be brought back.

Joy's former boyfriend, Paul, turns up at the house to return items which belong to her (p. 210). She is composed and the pair have a civilised – if slightly awkward – conversation (pp. 212–13). She knows that this will probably be the last time that she will see Paul as he is about to get married. Only when Paul has gone does Joy lose her composure. She is trying hard not to bottle up her feelings and lets out a cathartic scream (p. 215).

Joy has four hours to kill before returning to Foresthouse. She decides to pay a visit to her cottage. Dampness has permeated the cottage and mould and decay creep up each wall. She makes a preliminary start at tidying the place up, investigating the mould before stripping wallpaper from the bedroom. As she leaves the cottage, Joy waves politely at the newsagent.

The third and final time we see Joy in Foresthouse we note that she is far more at ease with herself and others, and a minor run-in with Janey (p. 220) fails to unsettle Joy. She realises that she cannot continue to adhere to the advice imparted in magazines because this type of literature does not speak to women like her. She resolves to stop reading trashy magazines and to start embracing her fears.

Joy has another dream about Michael. In this dream he undergoes a second more peaceful death. In a third dream occurring a few pages later there is clear distance between Michael and Joy. She asks him when she will be allowed to die and he laughs at her (p. 226). This is the final dream about Michael and one which allows Joy to say farewell to her lover. Following this dream, Dr Two informs Joy that she should be able to go home for Christmas.

Joy tries to take control of her situation by making important life decisions for herself. She has decided that she would like to leave hospital and that the agency should sell the cottage. Whilst she is unsure if these are the correct decisions to be making, she is satisfied that she is being proactive. Later,

when she is in a bar with her friends, Mhairi and Sam, she
encounters Norma Fisher. Joy realises that she and Norma
are equally afraid of each other. Rather than try to engage
Norma in a discussion in order to gain her forgiveness, Joy
leaves the bar (p. 230). She has a flashback to the tender
moments she shared with Michael before he died.

There is renewed hope in Joy as she returns to the house.
She transforms her image by cutting off her hair and bleach-
ing it. She cleans the house from top to bottom, indicating her
desire for a fresh start. Joy adds a festive touch to the house
by setting up fairy lights and tinsel (p. 234). She listens to
a Debussy cassette on her Walkman. As she listens to the
music she decides that she will learn how to swim, and
she remembers a maxim that she has heard before about
swimming: 'the trick is to keep breathing'. This resonates with
Joy's own situation – her life must go on. The tape winds to
an end and Joy admits that she has forgiven herself (p. 235).
The intense burden of guilt which she has harboured since
the beginning of the novel has, in part, lifted and her
rehabilitation will continue.

3. NARRATIVE STYLE

Narrative style is one of the most distinctive features of this novel. Galloway's experimentation with genre, structure and typography (the layout of text on the page) allows us to hear Joy's version of events as she interprets them, but also affords us glimpses of the world, as Joy experiences it. We might note the irony of the character's name; Joy is anything but joyous in this novel and it is possible to read her surname, Stone, as another pun. In the course of the novel, Joy develops an eating disorder and it is perhaps the measurement of weight – stones – to which her surname refers.

The Trick is a one-woman confessional novel. This is Joy's story and events are filtered through her (often skewed) perspective. With her opening words, Joy claims that she 'can't remember the last week with any clarity' (p. 6), immediately establishing Joy as an unreliable narrator. Later, Joy concedes that she is 'a liar and a cheat' (p. 95), reinforcing her status as a capricious storyteller. More subtly, Joy's trustworthiness is undercut by Galloway's decision to have her work as a drama teacher. Here is a character making a living from teaching others how to act. The generic fluidity of Joy's narrative – where the text transitions from conventional prose into snippets of reported speech, pages of scripted dialogues, dramatic monologues and short comedic sketches – makes it difficult to work out when Joy is, and is not, 'acting'. From the beginning of the novel we are primed by the author not to trust the narration of this complicated speaker, who is simultaneously witty and despondent; candid and dishonest; obsessive and blasé; analytical and negligent. For Galloway's protagonist, the figurative and literal 'trick' in life 'is to keep breathing'; for the reader of this novel, the trick is to keep re-reading a fragmented narrative in order to establish the fact within its many fictions.

With the deterioration in Joy's mental health comes an inability to describe or recall events coherently. Occasionally, we hear several very different versions of the same basic story. In a key scene where Joy is discussing her attempts to

conceal her affairs from Paul she states: 'I started writing my
diary in code' (p. 42). Following an episode in which she suffers
an anxiety attack and has to be sedated by a Foresthouse
nurse, Joy revisits the subject of the coded diary. In this later
interpretation, Joy implies that she had tried to read Michael's
diary when they lived together but was thwarted as it 'was
indecipherable [...] he wrote it in code' (p. 190). It is difficult
to believe that Joy and Michael both kept diaries in which
they veiled their secrets in code. We are disinclined to believe
that Michael's coded diary exists when Joy admits that when
she was a teenager her 'mother used to go looking for [her]
diary [...] One day what she read made her burn it' (p. 189).
We assume that the telling of truth has landed Joy into trouble
in the past, and she has been forced to become a skilful
editor of the truth. When living with Michael she keeps a less
than discreet 'red diary as big as a roadmap by the bedside'
(p. 190), almost willing Michael to read her fidelity to him.
Episodes such as these serve to remind readers that Joy's is
a mind in breakdown; this is a character that will say and do
anything to be liked, and anything to deny the magnitude of
her problems.

Despite the inaccuracies in Joy's narration, she does exhibit
an incredible 'with-itness' for someone battling depression
and breakdown; her sardonic wit and acerbic observations on
life, relationships, and society cut through even the darkest
moments. This brand of honesty keeps the reader sympatheti-
cally yoked to the main protagonist; we are willing her on to
succeed in her recovery.

4. THEMES IN THE NOVEL

The female struggle over male authority

In *The Trick*, Galloway explores the female struggle to assert power in patriarchal structures. In this respect, the late 1980s setting of the novel is significant. From 1979 to 1990 the United Kingdom had its first female Prime Minister, Margaret Thatcher (d. 2013). Thatcher was a divisive public figure. Her uncompromising style of leadership over Britain – and her predominantly male cabinet – won Thatcher the nickname 'Iron Lady'. Thatcher's now infamous refusal to do a 'U-turn' on policy ('you turn if you want to, the lady's not for turning') epitomised Thatcher's strong will in the face of opposition, and many of Thatcher's policies on social welfare proved unpopular. It is onto this backdrop that Galloway inserts her main protagonist, Joy Stone. It is surely no coincidence that the weak-willed, socially immobile female protagonist is the antithesis of all that Margaret Thatcher and her government were seen by many to represent. Joy is set up as a victim of the crumbling social welfare system run, chiefly, by men; she is victimised by her male bosses, and receives little assistance from the local authority housing office. In hospital, Joy is largely dismissed or patronised by male doctors or nurses.

At a time when the government was encouraging Britain to become a home-owning democracy through a 'right to buy' scheme, Galloway's protagonist lives in the house rented from the local Housing Authority. She is without the economic means by which to live comfortably in the property, let alone by which to purchase it. This property, which sits in the middle of a dilapidated housing estate ('Every fourth house in this estate is empty', p. 18), is in a state of utter disrepair ('The carpet is ancient [...] The threadbare bits are charcoal [...]', p. 7). This is not a desirable neighbourhood, yet Joy must negotiate with the Housing Agency to be allowed to stay there. Michael's name is on the lease; Joy has no legal right to live there given that she was neither a tenant nor married to the deceased. The man from the agency – satirically dubbed

15

'Mr Dick' by Joy for his overbearing officiousness – wants
her to know her place and relishes the opportunity to enforce
the rules:

> [...] Mr Dick said there were difficulties in my getting tenancy.
> They have to make a fuss so you know who's boss. There
> were rent arrears. I wasn't liable but Mr Dick explained if I
> paid them it might ease the aforementioned difficulties. I
> said I hadn't got the money.
>
> Mr Dick looked me right in the eye.
>   Try to be a little more co-operative. We're bending over
> backwards [...] We needn't do anything at all, strictly speaking
> [...]. (p. 18)

Knowing that Joy is desperate, Mr Dick attempts to manipulate her into paying off the debts, insisting that she ought
to be grateful that the Agency has not yet thrown her out onto
the street. With nowhere else to go, and no-one else to turn
to for financial or legal assistance, Joy must comply with Mr
Dick's unfair rules.

Many of Joy's difficulties stem from a distinct lack of
support from the male-led authorities. This is exemplified by
the seemingly substandard treatment Joy receives from the
National Health Service. She is aware that she is not being
paid adequate attention by her GP, Dr Stead. As the name
would indicate, he sends a health visitor *in his stead* to see
Joy: 'He said she [...] would find me out and let me talk. *Make
me* talk' (p. 20). Presumably, it is not the male doctor's place
to talk to women, or even to listen to their problems, but
only to diagnose. Joy's exclamatory response to this idea –
'HAH' (p. 20) – reveals to the reader her increasing sense of
detachment from this world she exists in. She finds it absurd
that the doctor believes the health visitor will force her to talk,
exactly at the moment in her psychological breakdown when
she is finding it difficult to admit the truth to herself. For fear
of being considered ungrateful she tries to convince herself
that '[...] Dr Stead was doing his best for me and that was

why [the health visitor] was here. I had to try' (p. 22). Later in the novel, when Joy is faced with a lack of personalised care in Foresthouse Psychiatric Ward, she must remind herself once again that 'hospitals are busy and under-resourced' and that she must 'try to be patient' (p. 110).

Joy rarely challenges authority but this does not mean that she is uncritical of those in power. We see this most notably through the pseudonyms she gives to male characters. Each doctor's real identity is concealed by Joy's decision to refer to him as 'Dr One', 'Dr Two', 'Dr Three' and so on. All of these doctors are, incidentally, male. This generic referencing system draws attention to the non-specific (and often useless) advice imparted by each of the doctors in turn. Joy is disdainful of their systems and procedures: her rendering of meetings in the form of dramatic scripts between 'DR' and 'PATIENT' reveals her awareness of the prescribed routines. During her first consultation at Foresthouse, Joy's cynicism is evident as she provides us with six lessons on psychiatrists:

> LESSON 1: Psychiatrists aren't as smart as you'd think. (p. 103)
> LESSON 2: Psychiatrists are not mind-readers [...]. (p. 103)
> LESSON 3: Psychiatrists give you a lot of rope knowingly. (p. 104)
> LESSON 4: Psychiatrists are just like all the rest. (p. 105)
> LESSON 5: Psychiatrists set thing up the way they want them. (p. 107)
> LESSON 6: Psychiatrists are devious and persistent. They always win in the end. (p. 108)

The doctors she encounters seem entirely contemptuous of her, not least when she has proactively made the appointments to speak with them about her situation. On two occasions Joy tries to take control of her situation to ask about the treatment she should be expecting to receive. On the first occasion, Dr Three entirely misreads Joy's motives for being there. He does not listen to her questions, and is not interested in talking with her. Instead, he offers Joy a weekend pass to go home.

When Joy protests that she doesn't 'understand any of this'
(p. 127) and that she feels pressurised into going home, Dr
Three terminates the conversation; the 'interview is finished'
(p. 127) without any questions having been answered.

At Joy's lowest ebb, she takes it upon herself to schedule
another meeting with Dr Three. She comes armed with three
suggestions for possible therapies – counselling, electrocon-
vulsive therapy (ECT) and analysis – but is instantly dismissed
by Dr Three as being 'ridiculous'. Joy comes to the realisation
that these men have no answers to her problems. Dr Three
implies that Joy should stop asking questions, and like Mr
Dick before him, suggests that Joy is ungrateful for their
assistance:

> You're getting the same treatment as everyone else. Rather
> better [...] Why don't you leave if you don't think we're doing
> you any good [...] Leave any time you like. Leave today. Get
> your bags and leave today. [This-will-teach-you-a-lesson.].
> (p. 164)

The parenthetical addition of 'this-will-teach-you-a-lesson'
serves as a reminder of Joy's ability to sift through their words
to find the truth. Sensing that his heart is not in the job,
she asks why Dr Three continues to undertake this line of
work. Seeing the balance of power shift in the conversation,
with the doctor becoming the patient, the doctor terminates
the discussion.

In a telling letter to Marianne, penned at the darkest point
in her breakdown, Joy conveys with clarity and concision the
futility of her experience at Foresthouse:

> I've seen three different doctors in the past fortnight, none
> twice.
> Dr Four says I need ECT, Dr Two thinks I need a good holiday
> and a career move, Dr Three thinks I take too much caffeine
> – a bit less and I'd be fine. Also a Dr Five turned up and
> suggested maybe we could have a chat. A CHAT [...] Yesterday

> Dr Four bumped into me in the corridor and didn't know who
> I was. It struck me after as pretty profound. (p. 179)

The lack of clear guidance is not what bothers Joy here, but
rather the fact that she has failed to make a lasting impression on Dr Four. Compare Joy's response to Dr Four's failure
to acknowledge her with her earlier anxiety about attending
the ward night out. Joy is adamant that she will not attend
the dinner dance. She lists her reasons (1: 'No-one will dance
with me', 2: 'No-one will [...] kiss me goodnight', 3: 'I will make
no-one's evening', p. 161). These reasons offer a telling insight
into how she views her role when it comes to men. She is there
to satisfy and to delight them.

Nowhere is this made more explicit than in her working
relationships with managers, Mr Peach and Tony. Our first
introduction to Mr Peach, the head teacher of Cairdwell
Secondary, comes when Joy is summoned to his office. Joy's
name for this written summons, delivered by a pupil and
penned on pink paper, is 'a billet doux' (p. 73), a French term
for an old-fashioned or jocular love letter. However, the nature
of the meeting with Peach – the discussion of a memorial
service for Michael Fisher – dramatically undercuts the notions
of *amour* set up by Joy's use of the loaded French phrase. Mr
Peach's news comes as a bombshell for Joy; the stress of
hearing Mr Peach's plans sends Joy into a frenzy, indicated
by the intrusion of text in the margins of the page. Just as Joy
has failed to foresee the contents of the note, so too does she
fail to comprehend why Mr Peach has asked to speak with
her. Simultaneously trying to mask her surprise, and provide
an 'appropriate' reaction to Mr Peach's news, Joy's response
– 'I appreciate being asked' (p. 73) – is pitched somewhere
between grateful and obliging. Yet, Mr Peach is not seeking
Joy's permission to go ahead with the ceremony, nor indeed
is he looking for her thanks; he is telling her in no uncertain
terms that a service will be going ahead, regardless of how
she feels. Joy's misery is compounded with the news that 'Mrs
Fisher will have to be invited. Of course' (p. 73). Mr Peach

confirms for Joy – as if further confirmation were required –
that she has no legal or social rights to try to counter Mr
Peach's plans.

A second meeting between the pair takes place chronologically after the memorial service for Michael, but before Joy
has described in detail the service itself. From the dramatic
dialogue (which takes the form of a staff appraisal between
BOSS and EMPLOYEE) the reader pieces together that Joy
has had cause to contact the Reverend Dogsbody, the man
charged with overseeing the school memorial service for
Michael. Mr Peach struggles to mask his contempt at his
employee's act of insubordination:

BOSS   You sent the Reverend Dogcollar a letter.
EMPLOYEE ....
BOSS   I think you show an unrealistic attitude. You,
            if anyone, should have been realistic.
EMPLOYEE Oh? [Dammit. He knew this one would get me.
            I can't keep silent much longer.] (p. 75)

Having suitably chastised his employee for daring to speak
out against his authority, Peach plays on his employee's
vulnerability by feigning concern for her welfare ('Now how
are you really?', p. 75). Under the guise of offering reassurance, Peach delivers the ultimate put-down: 'I want you to
know nobody thinks you're going off your head' (p. 75). Peach
shames Joy into submission, telling her that she will 'antago-
nise people' (p. 75) if she does not 'make an effort' (p. 75) to
look as though she is coping. As the meeting draws to a close,
Mr Peach commands Joy to 'smile'; he wants her to 'look happy',
to maintain a façade of wellbeing in the workplace, even if she
feels the very antithesis.

In the male-dominated world of the bookmaker's, Joy is
required to conform to 'feminine' type by smiling at inappropriate jokes ('This whore goes to the priest [...] This man
hasn't had sex for ages [...]', p. 31), and by only ringing up 'the
slips and check[ing] in winners' (p. 31). Outwardly unable to

challenge the behaviour displayed towards her by the men in charge – she simply cannot afford to lose either of her jobs – we are left with Joy's bitingly sardonic interior monologues which give us more accurate indicators of the character's true feelings: 'Sometimes I ring up the wrong thing and the men have to be patient with me' (p. 32). The sarcastic tone conveys Joy's utter disdain for the system she is trapped in. Joy acknowledges how the men 'nod in a longsuffering way among themselves [...] They are reassured by my ringing up wrong numbers' (p. 32). There is the suggestion in Joy's acknowledgement that she is perhaps doing the men a favour by intentionally ringing up the wrong numbers now and again, giving them reassurance of their superiority and her inferiority. From Joy's interactions in the bookmakers it is clear that Joy is anxious never to enact acts of insubordination towards her male superiors, even if she is chronically uneasy about the situations into which she is forced.

Femininity

Throughout the novel, Galloway places Joy in a number of scenarios where she threatens, transcends, or subverts societal codes of traditional 'femininity'. Joy claims that 'Afternoon is easiest' (p. 24) because the routines that she has established at this time of day allow her to most convincingly conform to society's stereotypical image of what women do. In the afternoon Joy goes shopping. She enjoys the sensuous experience of the supermarket and feels comfortable perusing the aisles of food. Joy is never lured into buying anything other than alcohol or baking ingredients to make cakes that she will never eat. Aside from alcohol, Joy's only other indulgences are magazines 'full of adverts and recipes, clothes and thin women [and] A new horoscope' (p. 25). Galloway draws attention to these apparent conventions of femininity when she describes Joy's almost ritualistic purchasing of her magazine. Having paid for it, Joy slips it carefully into her 'shoulder bag' before clicking along the precinct in her high heels (p. 25) to pore over the magazine's contents at home.

Later, as Joy prepares to commit suicide, she reflects upon the irrational hopes and fears cultivated in women by mainstream media and popular culture, a value and belief system that she has wholeheartedly bought into through her avid consumption of magazines. Joy conned herself into believing that if she waited long enough she would finally uncover the 'trick' to the ideal of 'happiness' projected by the magazines she reads. Joy provides a list of potential scenarios that she once believed would lead her to personal contentment:

> ie when
> – I get away from my mother
> – when I live with the man-I-love
> – when I get away from the man-I-love
> – when my mother loves me more
> – anyone loves me more
> – when I finish the diet/buy new clothes/get a haircut/buy new make-up/learn to be nicer/sexier/more tolerant/turn into someone else. (p. 193)

Over time, as she experiences disappointment after disappointment, Joy has had to modify this list. The hyphenated term 'man-I-love' conveys Joy's sarcasm at having once placed faith in such a childlike cliché. Repetition of the same term in the next line sees this sarcasm develop into bitterness at the failure of a series of relationships. Her grand dreams of finding a 'perfect' partner and settling down are dashed, as is her desire to have a better relationship with her mother. In Joy's tragic quest to find anyone to love her more she tries out various ways of making herself more attractive. The final point on the list is a selection of steps taken by Joy to improve herself. The first four options are cosmetic in nature (dieting, new clothes, haircuts, make-up) and are related to Joy's physical appearance. The next three deal with Joy's personality. Learning to be 'nicer' and 'more tolerant' seem reasonable objectives for Joy but the belief that she must be 'sexier' implies that she is seeking to gratify men. The series of options climaxes with the phrase 'when I [...] turn into someone else' (p. 193). Having exhausted all other avenues we must presume that Joy has given up on herself.

Within the magazine's pages Joy finds tips on how to be the 'perfect' housewife, and spends a great deal of time intricately describing domestic chores she undertakes. By talking us through cleaning and baking routines in such detail Joy attempts to prove her credentials as a 'good wife going to waste' (p. 41). She can enact – and enact to a high degree of success – the traditional roles of the female. Having lost her lover, she cannot prove to him that she would have made a good wife; however, she can prove it to herself and to others. She admits that she 'can't stop getting frantic about the house being clean and tidy for people coming' (p. 18). Like her own personal hygiene routines, Joy's cleaning regime is meticulous. She cleans the kitchen until her hands 'are swollen from cold water, red as ham' (p. 18) and the 'kitchen looks like they do on TV and smells of synthetic lemons and wax' (p. 18). On Sundays, Joy bakes. However, Joy is baking for no-one. In doing an activity deemed traditionally 'feminine', Joy is also aligning herself with Ellen, the mother of her best friend Marianne. Ellen is an efficient homemaker who tries to subject Joy to nourishing home-cooking and kindness. In light of Michael's death Joy asks Marianne what she will do to fill the loneliness whilst she is 'lasting'. Marianne provides Joy with a list of activities for Joy to try, each activity in some way associated with the 'feminine' or the role of the housewife.

Whilst many of the magazine articles and horoscopes she reads offer Joy the opportunity to indulge in escapist fantasies of domestic bliss, the letters on the problem pages confront Joy with some uncomfortable home truths, as mothers share concerns about their sons, and wives (or ex-wives) share anxieties about marriage. Aspects of these women's problems resonate clearly with Joy in her current situation: '[I] let the tears drip onto the rug until I'm ready to move up to the kitchen for some paper towels' (p. 28). The advice imparted by the 'agony aunt' acts as a substitute for female companionship.

As Joy is preparing to commit suicide, she reflects on where she has gone wrong in life, and magazines come under some harsh scrutiny:

> I spent a lot of time spending time. Magazines told me to work on my awareness. I would wake up and think this is my One Shot at Today. I'm Young, Dynamic, Today's woman. I'm multi-Orgasmic. I have to Live Life to the Full. I didn't know what this meant but I thought it anyway [...] I would get anxious if I hadn't done something new, discovered something, found a direction for my life. (p. 193)

The magazine headlines are here chanted like mantras, suggesting Joy's belief in what she was reading. As Joy comes to accept that life can go on without Michael, and without her mother, she accepts that she needs 'to stop reading these fucking magazines' (p. 223).

As Joy's relationships continually fall short of the 'ideal' peddled by magazines, she becomes afraid to walk away from loveless relationships. As the novel draws towards its conclusion, Joy admits that she did not fear being alone, but rather feared how people might judge her for being alone: 'too ashamed I wasn't fit to live with' (p. 42). Joy is afraid to split with Paul, not because of the hurt she will experience by not being with him any more, but because of societal attitudes about the breakdown of relationships. Attempting to excuse her actions, Joy claims to have stayed with Paul in order to protect her dying mother from finding out the truth, and as Joy grapples to overcome her depression, this notion is dismissed as nothing more than 'a romantic idea' (p. 42).

If the memory of her mother continues to plague Joy, then so too does the fact that she is in her late twenties, unmarried and childless. There are both subtle and explicit references to childbirth peppered throughout, and, although Joy never overtly addresses her state of 'childlessness', it is clear that this issue plays on her mind. We first notice this trope as Joy describes walking through the corridors at school:

> As you go upstairs you pass a painting of some kind of fantasy
> domestic scene: a whole house painted in poster colours with
> mummy in the kitchen and dad in the garage while a variety
> of offspring lie in bed or watch tv or play on a snake-green
> lawn. (p. 11)

The simple gesture of acknowledging this childish painting
betrays many of Joy's real emotions. Firstly, Joy has been
partly responsible for the breakdown of Michael's family unit
through their affair. Secondly, in her current state – where
she has lost her lover and is abusing her body to the point
where she might be unable to conceive children herself – she
sees this child-like rendering of domestic bliss as 'fantasy'.
The word choice is significant: in Joy's experience, real family
life is nothing like this idealistic or false portrayal. There is
a bitter edge to her tone as she uses the choice of the word
'offspring' to describe the children inhabiting the scene. The
word distances Joy from the image that she is viewing in order
to suggest that it does not bother her. With the inclusion of
this small episode, Galloway also reinforces the societal roles
(the mother and the wife) that women are supposed to play.
Other references can be found throughout. For example, Joy
currently lives in a house with four rooms which she concedes
is 'too big really' (p. 19). The council house is designed for a
family unit, not a single woman. Even as Joy makes herself
a cup of tea she considers the irony of her 'Family Size Economy
Green Label (Strong) Tea' (p. 17); she admits to having 'no
entitlement to a family-size box but it cuts costs' (p. 17). Joy's
use of the word 'entitlement' shows that she considers herself
to be in some way undeserving of the teabags because she has
no-one to care for or to share them with.

Issues of motherhood and maternity become a very real
concern for Joy when a consultant from Foresthouse ('a
real one', p. 140) suggests that Joy's failure to menstruate
may be as a result of her being pregnant. Joy dismisses the
idea through typically sardonic humour ('I don't menstruate.
I gave it up to save money', p. 140), but the doctor's reprimand

('I laughed and he told me to stop being silly', p. 140) humil-
iates Joy and forces her to face the stark possibility that she
could well be with child. Waiting for the scan to show on screen
Joy almost wills herself to be pregnant in order to feel in
some way alive:

> It wasn't swollen but so what. Maybe I really was pregnant.
> We might be doing more than discovering I exist: someone
> else might exist in there too. I scoured the screen looking for
> something sure to surface out of the haze on the monitor [...]
> [...] I looked. I was still there. A black hole among the green
> stars. Empty space. I had nothing inside me. (p. 146)

With the news that she is not pregnant, Joy seems, finally, to
give up on herself. Her body is a 'black hole' and her soul is
equally devoid of hope and (ironically) joy.

We know that this character is an adept actress, as she
readily assumes the various roles of the teacher, the lover,
the patient, the housewife and the 'other' woman; however,
here we see that playing the mother is the only female role
that Joy cannot readily 'perform'. Motherhood eludes her. In
this respect we might say that the novel is haunted by the
absence of mothers. As with Michael's death, the circumstances
of Joy's mother's death are hinted at – but not fully established
– until the middle of the novel. When asked by Dr One to
explain what Joy thinks is making her 'feel bad' (p. 103), she
begins her narrative by saying 'my mother walked into the
sea' (p. 104). The reader is momentarily misled into thinking
that Joy's mother has committed suicide by intentionally
drowning, but, as we learn, her mother did not actually die
from this episode. She died later, in hospital. Much of Joy's
deep sadness, it seems, stems from a fractured relationship
with her mother.

Joy's problematic relationship with her mother is nothing
in comparison with her problematic relationships with men.
Dressing for her shift in the bookmakers, Joy confesses:
'I dress with great care in front of the mirror. On Saturday I
work with men' (p. 30). She performs this careful dressing

ritual in an obligatory fashion as though she is expected to make the effort for the men with whom she works. This careful presentation of the self extends from her physical appearance to the manner in which she conducts herself in front of the punters: 'I'm supposed to smile and I do' (p. 33). Joy is aware of how women are viewed, particularly in the ultra-masculine setting of the bookmakers; although disdainful, she does nothing to counter it.

Joy Stone is not an instantly 'likeable' character, and her self-obsession borne largely from her depression makes it difficult for the average reader to connect with her. For much of the novel Joy is in self-destruct mode: she drinks too much; she neglects her health and wellbeing; she allows herself to be used by men; she uses men for her own gain; she withdraws from society; she refuses the help and advice of those around her; and she is inwardly disdainful of other women. As we get to know more about the character, however, we become more sympathetic towards her. For every withering or disparaging thought she passes about those trying to help her, she partly recognises aspects of the good in what they are doing. Joy has dangerously low self-esteem and many of her seemingly irrational actions stem from the desperation to be liked, and even loved. Joy places value on the intangible – astrology and horoscopes, dreams, fantasies, fictions, and agony aunt advice. Seeking validation for her actions, and confirmation that she is doing things 'properly', Joy turns to trashy magazines to show her how to be a 'woman'.

Grief and bereavement

One of the key functions of this novel is to explore the intense emotional burden of grief on the bereaved. The death of Michael Fisher is a recurring nightmare for Joy; in a series of flashbacks she sketches things both half-remembered and half-forgotten about the day Michael died and the hours leading to his death. Given that the details provided by her seem blurred, ambiguous, or even repeated for no immediately obvious reason, the flashbacks make it clear that Joy cannot accept that Michael is no longer with her. She is fixated with remembering the minutiae of the day itself, but she never states explicitly what has happened to Michael, and the reader is left to piece the story together.

In the flashbacks, Joy documents her own reactions towards the people she encounters in the immediate aftermath of the accident; her encounter with a young Spanish boy leaves a lasting impression on her, as she flashes back to it on more than one occasion. This episode has added poignancy as it is the young boy who inadvertently breaks the news of Michael's death to Joy. In the final flashback, we are poolside with the couple just as Michael has decided to go for a swim. We conclude that his death occurred moments after this final exchange. In the present, Joy does not talk to anyone about Michael. This inarticulacy means that her grief has no outlet. Her flashbacks are the medium through which she rationalises – and therefore begins to come to terms with – Michael's death.

Although Michael's death appears to have been the catalyst for Joy's present anguish and anxiety, we realise that Michael's passing is not the only significant loss that Joy has experienced in her life. Joy's narration leads us to conclude that her absent mother might have taken her own life, an ambiguity which is not clarified until much later in the novel. Despite Joy's reluctance to deal with the death of a loved one, it is apparent that her mother's death has had a profound impact on her. When Myra, Joy's formidable older sister, turns up unexpectedly, we realise that Joy did not allow herself to grieve properly. As the two women get drunk, Myra decides to reprimand her younger sister. With an incredible bitterness, Myra verbally attacks Joy for her failure to express any emotion on the day of their mother's funeral. Noting how Joy appears to be mourning deeply the loss of her married lover, Myra questions angrily: 'What about your mother you callous bitch? Never gret for your mother' (p. 67). The accusation levelled by Myra unsettles Joy and she has no response to Myra's question. Not until Joy contemplates taking her own life do we fully understand the circumstances in which Joy's mother died. Joy explains how her mother 'walked into the sea' (p. 199). This, as Joy notes, was not the first time that her mother had made an attempted bid at suicide and failed. Her mother died, having knocked her head at home following a fifth heart attack, heart attacks which were brought on by the strain of having 'walked into the sea'. It is difficult not to draw comparisons between Michael's drowning and Joy's mother's attempt to drown herself and the prevalence of water (dealt with in the **Symbolism** chapter of this Scotnote, p. 47), suggests this to be a connection that Joy herself has made on some level. At the end of the novel, as Joy attempts to rebuild her life, she resolves to learn to swim (p. 235). It is only here, in Joy's final resolution, that the significance of the book's title – *The Trick is to Keep Breathing* – becomes clear.

In Foresthouse, Joy seems resigned to the fact that there might not be any answers, that 'This is the Way Things Are Now' (p. 169). Joy is finally offered some assistance from Dr Two in the form of a self-help book, entitled *Courage and Bereavement*. Dismissing her initial scepticism ('The wrapper is purple with doves and clouds, warm and flaccid from his inside pocket', p. 170), Joy admits that she 'read the book in two and a half hours and [cried] all the way through' (p. 172). Although the advice imparted in this book is relatively common-place – be patient, seek the company of friends and family, laugh, pray – it resonates with Joy. Through reading this book, Joy comes to some awareness that she is grieving, but knowledge of her condition is not enough to cure it. Joy is not ready to begin the healing process and she deteriorates further before beginning on her road to recovery.

Guilt

The reason that Joy cannot accept the death of her lover is, in part, to do with the guilt she feels for being in some way 'culpable' for Michael's death. Joy and Michael's relationship began as an illicit affair whilst Michael was still married to Norma. Full of remorse, Joy tolerates more than she ought to from Norma, from Norma's lawyer, from her boss at work, and from Tony, believing that she does not deserve happiness. When Myra interrogates her on how she came to be in possession of the house, Joy remembers how '[she] had

no entitlement. He was married' (p. 62). She fixates on the
legalities. Even though Joy and Michael were cohabiting at
the time of his death, it is his estranged wife who is entitled
to Michael's estate in the eyes of the law. Joy's overwhelming
shame, combined with a fear of confrontation, means that she
will not publicly contest this accepted point of view. Joy's inner
monologue is effective in conveying her utter contempt for the
system in which she is trapped. Describing the messy dissol-
ution of Michael's estate Joy notes how 'his wife was kind
enough to let me have all this crap she didn't want' (p. 63).
There is no denying the bitterness in Joy's tone, but Joy is
still plagued with too much guilt to allow the bitterness to
take over. She feels she owes a debt to Norma:

> There's something I'd like to know, [Norma] said, and waited
> [...] When did it start? We both knew exactly what it meant.
> There was no mistaking [...] It was nobody's business but
> mine and it was also irrelevant. But I answered. [...] Twelve
> forty-five [...] Maybe I thought I owed her something.
> (p. 144)

Driven by the guilt of having started the affair at school,
Joy answers precisely to the minute, as though specificity
would make it easier for Norma to accept the deceit. Norma's
response – 'At least now I know. You told me something he
never would' (p. 144) – makes Joy feel as though she has
betrayed Michael.

A further sign of Joy's guilty conscience is her regular diary-
keeping. Joy admits that she took to keeping a diary during
her relationship with Paul, an indicator that her relationship
had its troubles. However, we quickly learn that this is not
the first time Joy has recorded her feelings in diary-form:

> When I was a teenager, my mother use to go looking for my
> diary. I'd find my underwear rearranged, too neat and know.
> [...] I was too stupid to stop writing [...] One day what she
> read made her burn it. (p. 189)

What possible revelation could Joy have included in her diary for her mother to have had such a hostile reaction to it? This significant episode from Joy's childhood is paralleled with an episode recounted from her time with Paul: 'A few months after he noticed it wasn't quite so available he hunted it down' (p. 189). Knowing that what she is divulging in her diary will cause upset in her relationship, Joy conceals it from Paul, just as she claims to have hidden her actions from her mother. There is a mutual distrust between Joy and Paul as we are led to believe that Paul had secretly been reading her diary; when access to her innermost thoughts and feelings are denied, Paul knows that Joy has been unfaithful. Later, Joy asserts: 'His own diary was indecipherable. He wrote it in code' (p. 190). We are left to wonder what the truth of the matter is. Has Joy purposely manipulated the episode to suit her narrative, or has her fragile state of mind caused her to forget the truth?

As the novel draws to its conclusion, Joy's feelings of guilt eventually begin to subside. As she makes the first tentative steps towards rebuilding her life, Joy finally listens to what her mind and body are telling her:

> The voice is still there.
> I forgive you.
> I hear it quite distinctly, my own voice in the empty house.
> I forgive you. (p. 235)

She has punished herself enough for the part she played in Michael's death. At the novel's end, Joy is not 'cured' of her depression, but is certainly in a much more optimistic frame of mind than she was when we first encountered her. Joy is ostensibly more positive and seems to have taken David's intervention in her suicide attempt as a sign that she was not ready to die. Rather than passively accepting her circumstances, Joy becomes proactive in the final pages of the novel. Her first step is to alter her image drastically; she cuts her hair 'spiky' with a set of dressmaking scissors before colouring it 'purple with permanent dye' (p. 232). She plans to pierce

her ears the next day. Joy scrubs her clothes, literally to
eradicate the sterile stench of the hospital from them, but also
metaphorically to wash away the memory of Foresthouse and
by extension the recent months of anguish. Joy tackles the
box marked 'DOVER PORT AUTHORITY' which contains
possessions shipped back from their ill-fated Spanish holiday.
Joy is defiant as she parts with the goods: 'the scent of
it makes me dizzy when I walk to the binstore. Nothing to do
with me any more' (p. 233). The very act of disposing of
these goods is testament to how far Joy has come since the
beginning of the novel.

Breakdown

The theme of breakdown is perhaps the most obvious theme
to identify, given that much of the novel's action centres around
a patient who has been admitted to the psychiatric unit
of a hospital and who attempts to take her own life in the
course of the novel. Further to Joy's psychological breakdown,
we find the breakdown or fracturing of her relationships, be
they platonic or romantic in nature. To aid her thematic
examination of breakdown, Galloway uses typography as a
clear indicator of Joy's state of mind. As her condition worsens,
the text fragments; thoughts trail off into nothing; vacant
space swallows the page. All of these typographical decisions
effectively convey the lack of cohesion in Joy's mind about
what has taken or is taking place in her life. Joy confesses to
the things that she can handle, and drip-feeds us information
on other aspects of her life which are often more important in
the context of the novel.

From the detached and paranoid narration of the opening
pages it is clear that Joy is not in a good way. She is barely
managing to keep control of her situation. Yet the worst is
certainly still to come. Melancholia festers within Joy and her
deterioration is rapid. Throughout, Joy is terrified to articulate
her own thoughts: 'I knew if I opened my mouth something
terrible would dribble out like the tea' (p. 22). She trusts no-one
enough to talk to them about her feelings but, perhaps more
importantly, Joy does not trust her own mind and therefore

cannot be sure how her innermost thoughts will be received by others. Joy goes to great lengths to perform 'sanity', but she is not always convincing. On her first meeting with the consultant at Foresthouse, we sense Joy's belief that she is in some way smarter than those professionals working in the institution to which she has been referred. The ecstasy which accompanies her having seemingly outsmarted the consultant ('I let my head hang back [...] The rush of blood made me abruptly dizzy [...] I was floating up towards the ceiling', p. 106) is undercut by the irony of Joy's line that 'the whole thing was insane' and the 'sardonic laugh' that she tries to affect. Joy attempts to look like a 'right-minded citizen worrying about her contribution to society' (p. 108) when she uses her job as an excuse not to come into the ward, but again this looks like the actions of a desperate woman.

Joy's desire to be seen as 'sane' is understandable, as are her concerns that she will lose control of her faculties. As Joy discusses her mother's death, she makes a telling admission that during her late mother's illness, her mother barely recognised her. Before swallowing the pills which she hopes will end her life, Joy ruminates on the idea that breakdown is a genetic problem. She describes how her maternal lineage is coloured with people who have attempted to take their own life. Thankfully, Joy escapes the same fate when she answers the door to David. However, this section of the novel shows how depression has ravaged Joy and driven her to the point where she wants to die. This is Joy's lowest ebb; from this point on, things can only get better.

Galloway does not afford Joy a miraculously quick recovery at the end of the novel, for this would feel contrived. Nonetheless, the reader is hopeful for her. It is clear that Joy wants to get better, even if she is not entirely sure about how, or when, this recovery might happen. As she sits contemplating the future, her resolution to take up swimming lessons shows the extent of Joy's personal progress. She knows that getting on with her life will require effort, willpower, and a lot more mistakes, but she will survive; she will keep breathing.

5. JOY'S RELATIONSHIPS

With men

Joy's relationship with Michael drives the narrative arc of breakdown and recovery. Yet this relationship, born from an illicit affair, is perhaps the most conventional (healthiest, even) of all of the relationships with men that Joy chooses to reveal to us. She reflects on the couple's attempts to foster a 'conventional' romance, but she also talks of a second, long-term, romance with Paul, a relationship allowed to stagnate by both partners. An ongoing problem for Joy is the amorous intentions of her boss at the bookmakers. Reluctant to engage with Tony on a sexual level, but anxious not to disappoint, Joy succumbs to his advances.

1. Tony

In Joy's eyes, Tony oscillates between the parodic, the predatory and the pathetic. It is clear that Tony is a man with an inflated sense of his own importance. Tony lusts after Joy. However, he (and his hot-blooded advances) are given short shrift as she struggles to keep him at arm's length. More widely, Tony exists as the epitome of the patriarchy that Galloway sets out to critique in the novel.

Preparing for her shift, Joy asserts: 'I dress with great care [...] On Saturday I work with men' (p. 30). Before we have even encountered Tony, it is clear that Joy's employer does not pay her to think. As the only female in the male-dominated realm of the bookies, Joy knows her function is largely aesthetic. She explains, 'I'm supposed to smile and I do' (p. 33); Joy is not there to question Tony's systems or his authority. Tony is extremely tactile with Joy, groping her at every given opportunity: 'He squeezed my hip when I laughed then told me I was too skinny. Look, see? squeezing my backside' (p. 173). Joy does nothing to encourage Tony, but to him, the fact that she does not prohibit his touch is encouragement enough.

Allan, a colleague of Joy's, claims Tony's greyhound receives 'more attention [from Tony] than he gives his wife' (p. 32).

Whilst Joy has 'never heard his wife's name' (p. 32) she is more than familiar with 'Tony's Queen', his prized greyhound. In Tony's world, women are subservient. The fact that Tony has concealed the name of his wife from Joy suggests that he has ulterior motives. Even Tony's greyhound has been given a name suggestive of Tony's ownership and power, and of female subservience. Galloway's playful semantic trickery runs throughout the novel, but in episodes such as this one, we see Galloway's mastery of acerbic wordplay as the author critiques male dominance. Tony's pastime gives us an adequate metaphor with which to describe Tony's pursuit of Joy, as though she is the rabbit luring the baying greyhound. He is shameless in his attempts to get Joy on a date, asserting 'I'll take you one day' (p. 32), in reference to the greyhound track. Joy is unenthused by the prospect but, unable to counter his advances, she instead tries to ignore what Tony is saying to her. There will be no contest in this race, however; Joy is unable to say 'no' or to articulate her feelings. Tony exudes an arrogance that overwhelms her.

Although relentless, Tony's methods in wooing Joy are laughably clichéd. In his initial flirtations, Tony positions himself as the chivalric hero – 'I don't get to put on my coat without [Tony's] helping hand' (p. 33). Later, as Tony attempts to impress Joy, he relishes playing the romantic lead in his own film. He serenades Joy with Dr Hook and compliments:

> *When you're in love with a beautiful woman, it's hard*
> He looks sidelong to see my reaction, encouraging me to be cute. He keeps doing it between sentences (p. 98).

Tony thinks he knows how this situation will play out; he also thinks he knows how Joy ought to act in this situation. His conception of 'dating' is informed by American culture, signalled by the Country rock music, and Joy signals her awareness of this through her use of Americanisms. When the appropriate reaction is not forthcoming, Tony offers Joy somewhat lame encouragement to be 'cute' (p. 98), suggesting that he desires her to be childlike and naïve in response to his flirtations.

Galloway is satirising the male gaze on the female. Joy is weighed up by Tony in the same terms by which he would measure the efficiency/potential for good performances from a greyhound, as he concludes, 'a few more pounds and you'd be a stunner' (p. 98).

Tony's hackneyed attempts at romance are undermined by the fact that he is married. Joy is conscious that she does not want to find herself in the position of 'the other woman' once more and poses the question to Tony: 'Won't your wife be wondering where you are?' (p. 100). Tony is momentarily stopped in his tracks, but his plans are not entirely scuppered:

> He held my chin and made me meet his eyes.
>   Promise we can do this again, he said. Promise me. I think
> I was smiling, not wanting to but not able to stop.
>   He said, I've never met anyone like you.
>
> He kissed me again before he went for the car and I came in
> and threw up like an animal. (p. 100)

Joy is not attracted to Tony; on the contrary, Tony repulses her. On a second 'date', the conclusion to the evening is more worrying. Tony invites himself into Joy's living room (p. 174), breaching Joy's boundaries; the outcome of this 'date night' seems inevitable as she admits: 'I didn't say no'. Yet, neither did she say yes. Sexual intercourse with Tony represents the unsettling climax to Joy's inarticulacy. As Joy tries to make her discomfort known Tony shuts her up: 'When I spoke he covered my mouth again, cigar smoke in his saliva [...] I undid the buttons myself to make it quicker [...]' (p. 175). This is uncomfortable reading. Tony wants Joy to express her pleasure ('Tell me you like it', p. 175) but certainly does not want to see or hear her pain:

> afterwards, he said he wished I had talked more. I should
> have spoken to him, said things. And shouldn't I stop crying
> now. He wiped himself down with his white handkerchief
> and told me it was all right now. Stop crying. He sighed [...]

He said I'd be fine after I'd had some sleep. I had too much
to drink. (pp. 175–76)

Joy is 'rewarded' by Tony for her compliance, and receives
'an extra fiver' in her next pay packet. Joy does not have to
elaborate. Her submissiveness during their sexual encounter
has been rewarded by Tony in monetary terms. Joy's body
is a commodity; she has been paid for her services, and
her silence.

2. Paul

It might be argued that Joy's long-term relationship with Paul
is her most significant, as it has the greatest impact on who
she is as a person. It is this relationship – spanning seven
years – which has cultivated her questionable conception of
what an adult partnership looks like. Paul and Joy's teenage
'fifth form romance' (p. 41) blossomed from the seeds of a
shared sense of rebellion: 'our first date was in a café when
we should have been in French' (p. 41). As a teenager, Joy was
much more outspoken than her boyfriend, and in one recol-
lection Joy remembers how she questioned the authority of
teachers as Paul remained silent. This defiance is noteworthy
for its contrast with Joy's much more subdued narrative voice
in the present day.

Joy glosses over the initial years of their cohabitation, but
lingers for a time on the gendered roles that they both seem
naturally to fall into. Gone is the teenage rebel, and in her
place stands the domesticated housewife: 'I learned to cook
good meals and run a house. The fridge was always well stocked
and the cupboards interesting […] but I knew there was something missing' (p. 42). By following the advice imparted by
'experts' in her magazines, Joy has made herself a domestic
asset to Paul – after all, what more could he possibly need
from a woman than what she could offer? Nonetheless, it is
Joy who is left dissatisfied with their relationship, seemingly
experiencing the proverbial 'seven year itch'. Joy believes
talking through their problems will lead to the answer, but
her efforts to engage Paul in a frank discussion about their

relationship are unsuccessful. Paul believed that intimacy,
rather than communication, was the problem: 'I thought the
answer was soul-searching and he thought it was split-crotch
knickers. Stalemate.' (p. 42) They have become 'stale' mates
rather than soul mates. The masculine response to the problem
is to try and inject passion into the relationship by means of
'sexy' underwear. We might infer from this that Paul believes
their problems exist because Joy is not appearing to make a
big enough effort to please him sexually.

Unable to make progress towards reconciling their differ-
ences, the pair grow increasingly distant from each other:

> He punished me for his unhappiness by refusing to touch
> me. Night after night. I punished him for my unhappiness
> by not speaking [...] His willpower lasted out for months.
> A year. More. Practice was making him perfect and me
> desperate for kisses. I had an affair. (p. 42)

Paul begins to read Joy's diary and soon finds out about
the affair. Paranoid, and unable to work out how Paul
managed to find out about it, Joy begins keeping her diary
in code. In her narration of the relationship's breakdown,
we also find evidence to suggest the fragility of her own
mental state:

> I was vastly inferior in every respect [...] I talked to myself
> more and more [...] We were killing each other. There was
> nobody to ask for help because I was too proud and too
> ashamed I wasn't fit to live with. (p. 42)

Despite Joy's stark realisation that both she and Paul are
trapped in a destructive relationship, Joy cannot find the
courage to make the break. She finds excuses – practical
reasons – for remaining with Paul; she continues to clean the
house and cook, and he, in return, offers Joy the services of
his car to visit her dying mother. On the day of her mother's
funeral, the pretence between the pair seems too obvious to
deny anymore:

> He shook my hand in line with everybody else waiting outside
> the crematorium. I looked at his face and couldn't think who
> he was for a minute. It didn't feel better when I remembered.
> It felt worse. (p. 43)

Going through the motions of passing on his condolences, Paul
gives no hint of the intimacy they once shared. Joy finds no
comfort in his touch, the thing she had longed to feel.

The relationship continues to groan under the weight of
deceit and distrust; Joy has yet another affair, whilst Paul
admits to having himself had numerous affairs. When
Paul defiantly asserts 'I don't need you for anything' (p. 43),
Joy is cut to the core. In this one sentence Paul steals Joy's
romantic *raison d'être* from under her feet – Paul can survive
without her being in the house. She is no longer of any use to
him and he is no longer physically attracted to her. As Joy
reflects on this volatile break-up she notes how 'These days
[Paul] stays away' (p. 44). Paul 'has someone else who cooks
his meals' (p. 44).

It is odd, therefore, that when Myra, Joy's domineering
sister, arrives uninvited that the first person Joy turns to for
assistance is Paul:

ME	It's OK, it's just me [...] Look, I know it's late but can you speak to me [...] there's nobody else to call [...]
PAUL	Listen. [...] What do you want?

[...] I play my ace.

ME	Myra's here.
PAUL	[Long silence]
ME	Paul? Myra's here.
PAUL	I know. She phoned and asked for your address. (pp. 67–68)

Paul's reticence to engage with Joy is understandable, given
the circumstances under which they broke up, and the fact

that he has a new partner. However, the short sentence
'I know' betrays Paul's guilt in the present matter and his
complicity in Myra's unscheduled visit to Joy. With such a
long history together as a couple, Paul is the only person
that Joy believes will understand the threat Myra poses.
When Paul hangs up, having declined to help, Joy is left
reeling. Paul has betrayed her and left her to face the consequences. Joy is the one who now needs Paul's assistance.

Joy informs us that, on the evening that Norma Fisher found
out about the affair between Michael and Joy, it was Paul
who, having only come round to deliver Joy's birthday present,
'cleaned up the mess, crying because I was' (p. 194). The
memory of that fateful evening moves Joy to pity 'poor Paul';
she admits to crying 'big tears' thinking about Paul and what
happened between them (p. 194). It is clear, then, as the novel
moves towards its conclusion, that Joy and Paul must have
one final confrontation in order for Joy to accept that they can
no longer be in each other's lives and for her to begin to accept
that her independence from men is a positive thing.

This final meeting comes directly after Joy has had a profound
dream about Michael, in which Michael's *distant back melts
into the woods* (p. 210). Her subconscious might be indicating
that time is approaching to say goodbye to the past but this
does not mean that the physical meeting between Paul and
Joy is any less painful. The inarticulacy which plagued their
relationship is present once more during their dialogue; Paul
cannot articulate what he has come to tell Joy – that he is
getting married – and Joy knows that if she talks 'straight he
gets flustered and runs away' (p. 212). Joy detaches herself
from the situation by turning their hesitant conversation into
another scripted exchange, this time between HARRIDAN
and EX. 'Harridan' is connotative of bossiness and belliger-
ence, and Joy's use of it here conveys her belief that she is
inferior or in some way repellent to Paul. The stage directions
excellently gloss the characters' feelings of exasperation. Joy
'Thinks about the times they said they'd always be friends
and how hopeful it seemed then' whilst Paul muses 'about the
times they said they'd always be friends and how naïve they

were then' (p. 213). Although she finds it difficult, Joy navigates the discussion, managing to keep it together. As Paul leaves she summons the courage to wish him well: 'Be happy [...] I hope you're both happy' (p. 215). Joy's pain at losing Paul from her life is palpable: 'I scream dammit. I scream' (p. 215). The 'dammit' is tinged with defiance, and a sense of catharsis. Joy's long-term relationship with Paul was characterised by distrust, lies and deceit. In Joy's interpretation of this relationship, both parties were equally to blame for its breakdown. Having realised this, and having bid a civilised farewell to Paul, Joy's journey to recovery can continue.

3. David

David's part within this novel is relatively minor in comparison to the roles played by Paul, Michael or Tony. Nonetheless, David serves an important function as he is Joy's one constant, the only person in her life on whom she seems able to depend. In Foresthouse, Joy displays a photograph of David on her locker. Another patient's enquiries about who this person is stimulate Joy's memories about how she and David first got together. Like her affair with Michael, Joy's relationship with David began at school; somewhat unnervingly, however, David was not a colleague of Joy's but rather a pupil at the school Joy worked in. Joy seems to understand the problematic nature of the liaison and takes full responsibility for the instigation of their affair:

> We did the *so what are you doing now* number for a while then he asked me how I was. He looked shy when I didn't get it. He wanted me to talk about my mother. We went for a drink [...] It was me who started it. I kissed his neck. Out of the blue. I started to undress him in the car. Paul was on some management course for work. (p. 131)

When Joy thinks about David she ponders: 'Maybe I was pretending he was Paul' (p. 131), as though David was a proxy for the teenage lover (and by extension the excitement) Paul once represented.

Unlike the doctors on the Foresthouse ward, David seems acutely aware of what has brought Joy to this point. In the immediate aftermath of Michael's death, Joy overhears a discussion between David and Marianne during which David pinpoints the problem: 'She shouldn't get dependent on any one person again. Not on one person' (p. 132). David's comments reach straight to the heart of this novel; whilst Joy Stone ostensibly seems to be living the life of an independent female, free from the apparent societal 'shackles' of motherhood and marriage, she is desperately dependent on prescription drugs, alcohol and various men to keep her balanced and seemingly 'normal'. Galloway uses the character of David to subtly draw attention to the theme of dependency. David recognises the need for Joy to stand on her own two feet, to not become so heavily reliant on men. When Marianne leaves for America and Sam departs for university, David continues to visit Joy. Against David's better judgement it appears that Joy has become dependent on David's company:

> Then he turned up at the house unexpectedly [...] David reached over and kissed me. I closed my eyes tight [...] When he stood up, I didn't say anything. Not till I was sure he would hold me some more with my eyes closed. I wanted it too much to risk being wrong. Afterwards I cried till I screamed [...] This is the pattern of what I do when I am with David. We get drunk and have sex and I scream a lot of the time. (pp. 132–33)

David is a safe lover for Joy in that she knows that he does not expect anything of her. He has seen Joy at her lowest ebb but remains loyal to her. It is this friendship that hauls Joy out from the depths of despair into which she has sunk towards the end of the novel.

As the pills Joy has overdosed on begin to take effect, and she swirls in and out of consciousness, a tap at the window stirs her senses. In her drugged state Joy is aware enough to realise that this tapping could be her lifeline; if she answers the door she has to accept that she does not truly want to die:

> Through the cloud there is someone looking in [...] I don't
> have to focus. David holds a bottle in one gloved hand. He
> mouths at the glass. Happy Birthday. (p. 203)

We have witnessed Joy's struggle throughout to find someone
on whom she can rely; David's timely arrival confirms to her
that she already has that dependable person in her life. Despite
their sexual relations, it is clear that David and Joy are not
destined to be romantically linked; however, their companionship is more valuable to Joy and exactly what she needs at
this stage in her rehabilitation.

4. Michael

Although Michael's death has been the catalyst for Joy's
breakdown, and memories of his final hours haunt her, we
nevertheless get the sense that this relationship might not
have been as entirely satisfying for Joy as we have been led
to believe. What starts out as an affair turns into something
much more acceptable when Michael is forced to move in with
Joy out of practical necessity after his wife uncovers his disloy-
alty. In Joy's retelling of events we sense that Joy is not entirely
comfortable with this forced cohabitation, and that it has come,
perhaps, too quickly in their relationship. There is also the
suggestion that the secrecy of the affair is what Joy enjoys;
living together renders a once exciting relationship prosaic.
Once again, the notion of dependency is broached when Joy
asserts: 'it was important that he had his own place so he
needn't feel dependent. Besides I didn't want anyone staying
with me out of necessity' (p. 65). On this occasion it is not Joy
who depends on the male, but rather the male who has a
socio-economic dependency on the female. Joy intimates that
she would not want Michael to feel enslaved by their relationship, or to feel that he owed her something. Michael has not
willingly left his wife and children to be with Joy; circumstances
have dictated that he needs to move in. In Joy's mind, there

is no proof that Michael genuinely wants to be there with her. Joy's behaviour with her long-term lovers is contradictory: with Paul she was desperate to find something – anything – that she could offer him that no other woman could in order that he might stay with her, but the opposite seems true of her relationship with Michael.

The balance of power in Joy's relationship with Michael quickly shifts, as his 'council application paid off' (p. 65). Having discovered dry rot at her cottage, Joy is forced to move into Michael's newly acquired council house. She notes how 'we shipped in the clothes from the cottage during the night' (p. 65), suggesting the covert nature of the operation. It seems that the lovers are still unwilling to broadcast their romance in public. Galloway's use of the possessive effectively conveys Joy's awareness of – and relative comfort in – her inferiority to Michael when in 'his house' cooking 'chicken in his oven' (p. 65). With the freedom to come and go as she pleases, Joy feels that she is the epitome of 'perfect' or 'independent' women promoted in her trashy mags. As Joy concedes, 'the magazines would have approved like hell' (p. 65). With Michael's passing it now seems that the house traps Joy. She feels as unwelcome in this rented accommodation as the spores which occupy her own cottage. On her return from Spain she removes the house number from the door (two different sets of the number thirteen, a portentous omen in Joy's mind), leaving two sets of holes. The holes metaphorically refer to the hole in Joy's life, created with Michael's unexpected and sudden passing.

Despite both partners being young professionals, Joy admits that they were suffering financially: 'Reckless, we booked a holiday we couldn't afford in Spain […] the money would turn up. His stars said so' (p. 65). Buoyed by Michael's horoscope prediction that sunshine would fix all his financial problems, Joy encourages him to book the ironically ill-fated Spanish vacation. Joy's insistence on the validity of horoscopes explains in part the heavy burden of guilt she bears about the tragic outcome of this holiday.

At Michael's burial, faced with Norma, the children, and the assembled mourners, Joy acts as she is 'supposed' to do.

Sadly, for Joy, the worst part of her 'endurance test' (p. 83) is yet to come. Following Michael's death, Joy's financial problems intensify. Nora Fisher is given first refusal of Michael's belongings and many items from the council house evidencing the shared domestic life of Joy and Michael. As Joy glibly notes, 'His wife didn't want them anyway' (p. 19). The items Joy is left with have a revealing narrative to tell: 'The Bowie poster hides wine stains where I threw a glass at the wall. A wee accident' (p. 19). Joy's unconscious revelation of the self continues as she suggests that there might have been problems in the relationship. The Bowie poster physically masks the mark left by Joy's hot-headed antics. The euphemistic phrase 'a wee accident' indicates Joy's attempts to lie to herself and to the reader. We might presume that there was nothing accidental about it. Yet, in the need to absolve herself of the mounting guilt she feels in relation to Michael's death, Joy cannot admit to herself that their relationship was anything less than idyllic.

With women

Many of the women Joy interacts with she does not, in fact, like. She endures a daily car share with nameless women from work, during which 'they never say much' (p. 13). More generally, inarticulacy is a characteristic of Joy's engagement with women. Later, with the female Health Visitor, Joy requires a pre-prepared scripted conversation to get her through the ordeal; the same technique is used again during a phone conversation between Joy and Myra which is set down in the form of a dramatic dialogue between the characters 'MYRA' and 'ME'. Whilst men make Joy uncomfortable, women scare her. For example, the Health Visitor is overweight and Joy obsesses over this woman's lack of control; her mother's suicide bids concern Joy for the fact that she might have inherited her mother's traits; her sister, Myra, is abusive; her best friend Marianne seems in complete control of her life, and this draws attention to the fact that Joy is not; Norma Fisher makes Joy feel guilty, but also anxious as she does not know what pain Norma might yet inflict on her as payback. Marianne's mother

Ellen, and psychiatric patients Norah and Ros, are the closest
Joy comes to having female 'friends' around her. Abstract
agony aunts and female contributors to problem pages serve
in some way as kindred spirits. During her breakdown, Joy
does not want friends around her. Advice given from someone
she does not have to talk/lie to (magazines or the self-help
book given to her in Foresthouse) is as much engagement as
she can tolerate during her illness.

6. SYMBOLISM

Water

Both of the significant personal tragedies suffered by Joy have been directly or indirectly linked to water. Whilst Michael died in a Spanish swimming pool accident, Joy's mother attempted (perhaps more than once) to take her own life by drowning herself. Thus, water has come to represent a destructive force in Joy's life, and references to water punctuate Joy's narrative. We are introduced to the grieving protagonist in the opening pages of the novel as she sits alone in the dark. Joy fixates on the 'blue shapes […] and green lines' of the threadbare carpet which are 'like seaweed', the bald patches on the carpet appear 'liquid black. Still wet', and the carpet seeps to the touch (p. 7). The furniture emerges from the darkness 'like bits of sunk ship rising out of the wash of green' (p. 7). In this opening sequence, water clearly poses a threat for Joy. 'Sitting in the armchair', Joy surveys her living room like a survivor surveying the site of a wreckage; we get the sense that, whatever Joy's current predicament, she is only just managing to remain afloat. Such vivid and unsettling imagery has a powerful effect on the reader; it implies Joy's sense of dislocation in familiar surroundings; it establishes the feelings of melancholy seeping into Joy's mind; and suggests that these thoughts are threatening to submerge the character.

Occurrences of water imagery are much more prominent as Joy's psychological wellbeing deteriorates and she is admitted onto the psychiatric ward at Foresthouse for a period of time (for example: 'I find my sea legs in the green and blue corridor', p. 115). During a rare ward night out, the patients are escorted by staff for an evening of drinks and dinner. In Joy's description of this outing, the dining space (or 'lagoon room') at the Goodwill Inn is 'turquoise with plastic waterlilies', whilst the 'stink of chlorine' (p. 167) is unmistakeable. Having been made to attend, Joy finds herself in a situation which is entirely beyond her control. This relatively formal dining experience poses numerous (very obvious) problems for Joy, who has

continued to starve herself in hospital and will now have
to go through the motions of eating a meal which is highly
calorific, and of paying the price later. The thought of being
exposed panics Joy, and she is wary of her unfamiliar surroundings. More than the aquatic colours of the room itself, the
clinical 'stink of chlorine' carries negative connotations with
its clear association with swimming pools. The anxiety caused
by yet another evening event on the ward – this time the
patients' Hallowe'en Party – culminates in Joy passing out,
presumably from starvation, but in the passage of prose
leading up to Joy fainting it is difficult to ignore the water
symbolism:

> There is blurry accordion music and nurses twirling under-
> water in the arms of these men. One hand has blue tattooed
> crosses on the knuckles. My ears swim to the Gay Gordons
> [...] MOIRA wobbles toward the table with a white plate, a
> potato and beans, a glass of emerald fizz.
>
> Enjoy yourself, she says, rippling as she walks away. My eyes
> water [...] The green lemonade hisses. I notice just before
> the table comes up to smack my cheekbone [...]. (pp. 117–18)

Weak with hunger, and struggling to remain in control, the
abundance of water imagery symbolises that Joy is figuratively
drowning on the ward.

Another place where water imagery is discernible is in Joy's
flashbacks to the day of the accident. The initial flashback
(p. 9) recounts the final minutes enjoyed by the couple. Michael's
first utterance in the novel – *'I'm going to swim'* (p. 9) – feels
ominous and the reader's feelings of foreboding are heightened
by the accompanying description of an inauspicious pool which
is *'very bright in the sun'* as *'ripples slither along the surface'*
(p. 9). Details of the accident scene which are shared in subse-
quent flashbacks convey just how haunted Joy is by what she
has experienced. She vividly remembers how a man attempting
to revive Michael's body resembled *'a whale hump of backbone
over someone lying on the tiles'* (p. 69); Michael's lifeless body

is covered '*with yellow bruises* [...] *neck chain filled with water like fish eyes fingers tinged with blue*' (p. 184). Even as Joy makes the first tentative steps toward recovery, the destructive potential of water and the sea is still a pressing concern for the novel's protagonist. In a poignant memory detailed towards the end of the novel, Joy remembers:

> *The night before he died we went walking along the sea.* [...] *We came back to sit by the poolside* [...] *Someone was swimming, slicing effortlessly like a shark into the tight black skin of the water* [...] *We looked out over the pool, the white arms of the swimmer rising and sinking out there in front of us. Just visible in the dark* [...]. (p. 231)

The image of the competent, shark-like swimmer, cutting through the darkness of the pool is easily read as an ominous portent of Michael's death. Yet, it is also symbolic of Joy's current state of mind, as she moves through and beyond the darkness of the depression which had taken over her mind and body in the months following the accident.

More and more, water comes to symbolise Joy's utter helplessness, both in the present and at the time of Michael's accident. In a passage where Joy describes her dependency on sleeping pills and tranquillisers and her attempts to convince Dr Stead to prescribe her drugs, Joy admits:

> Poor Dr Stead. I don't tell him the half of what I do. I'm a liar and a cheat with Dr Stead while he sees endless queues of sick people and tries to make room for me. I watch the swans and they watch me, useless at the edge of the water with nothing to give. Eventually they give up interest altogether and drift further downstream. (p. 95)

As she watches the swans, Joy's subconscious makes links, once again, to Michael's death, as she stood beside the pool, powerless to help her lover. The final sentence here is revealing: the swans symbolise her past partners, who have grown bored of Joy. We might also read that she feels that she has nothing to offer men, who will always eventually grow bored and seek whatever they are looking for elsewhere.

Although water can be read as destructive or dangerous, it might also be argued that water symbolises regeneration. In the morning, Joy performs 'function washes, not full ritual' (p. 10), a quick wash 'taking the sweat of the night' – and the nightmarish memories which plague her – 'away' (p. 10). These washes are suggestive of Joy's lack of care. A longer soak requires much more time and effort and this type of careful washing usually occurs when Joy has planned an encounter with a man. However, as the novel progresses, Joy's bathing habits are carried out almost ritualistically. In a section subtitled *The Bathing Ritual* (p. 46), Joy outlines with exact precision the lengths she takes to get ready for a night out:

> The bathwater must be hot: warm isn't good enough [...] I pour oil into the scalding water. My skin gets creaky and dry as I get thinner, like tracing paper [...]
> On the white bath rim, the wash glove
> > the soap.
>
> [...]
> When I finish, the skin sizzles: my whole surface sings. I stand up in the bath draining away the ordinariness that floats with the scum on the water [...]. (p. 46)

Joy is transformed and rejuvenated by this routine which takes in every aspect of her body, from head to toe. As Joy adorns her newly cleansed body with lotions and perfumes it is clear that she is preparing her body to be gazed upon and touched by the male who will arrive shortly. In equal measures Galloway seems to be using Joy as a mouthpiece through which to both critique and appreciate the craft of being female. Joy tints her cheeks a shade called 'Peaches and Dream' and opts for a clear wax on her lips rather than a vivid red which 'leaves marks' (a sure sign that whoever Joy is meeting that evening is in a relationship already). Despite the hours of careful preening, 'the woman in the mirror [...] is never what I want [...] Someone [...] too much like me' (p. 48). The new day will bring yet another function wash to remove the memory of the evening before.

At the novel's end, Joy's decision to learn to swim suggests a real desire to overcome her fear of water:

Maybe

Maybe I could learn to swim.
[...]
I'm gawky, not a natural swimmer. But I can read up a little, take advice. I read somewhere the trick is to keep breathing, make out it's not unnatural at all. They say it comes with practice. (p. 235)

In this respect, mastery of the act of swimming and, by extension, a newly acquired ability to navigate water, could be Joy's salvation. She will not make the same mistake as Michael. She will not drown.

The colour red
The colour red permeates this novel, from the red pills given to Joy to combat her depression; to Michael's red mouth; to the blood shed as Joy cuts herself. When Joy's periods cease owing to severe weight loss, blood is conspicuous in its absence. Following an unsettling visit from the health visitor, during which she did not 'perform' to the best of her ability, Joy fixates upon 'one of the red cups' in her kitchen which has 'a hairline crack along the rim' (p. 24). Joy throws this mug away, not because it is broken and she might accidentally hurt herself on it, but because she is worried that 'the person that it cuts is not me' (p. 24). The cup is here personified, as though the cup, and not the person wielding it, is the true threat to Joy's safety. Joy cannot trust herself not to hurt herself and so throws the cup away. Here, the red mug symbolises Joy's desire to self-harm.

Describing the moments during which she realised that she did not miss her skipped meal, the colour red figures regularly:

> There was a can of vegetable soup in the cupboard [...] I
> found the opener and dug it into the top [...] Some of the
> stuff inside smeared on my knuckle [...] Inside the can the
> surface was a kind of flattened jelly, dark red with bits of
> green and yellow poking through [...] I slid one finger into
> it [...] The top creased and some of the pink fluid slopped up
> and over the jagged lip of the can. It was sickening but
> pleasantly so [...] the torn rim scored the skin [...] Soup stung
> into the cuts so I [...] scooped up as much mess as I could
> and cradled it across the room, red soup and blood dripping
> onto the lino [...] I was learning something as I stared at
> what I was doing; the most obvious thing yet it had never
> dawned on me [...] I didn't need to eat. (p. 38)

The sight of her own blood confirms to the narrator that she is indeed alive, despite not having eaten. There is a pleasure in exerting pain on herself; starvation and self-harm become ways in which Joy can remain in control of her situation. When Joy's periods stop, the possible implications of this change in her bodily cycle – pregnancy, and her lack of control over the situation – terrify Joy.

References to the colour red proliferate when Joy's breakdown is at its height. Joy refers to her medication as 'THE RED THINGS'; the 'silent spores' devouring the cottage are described as 'the creeping red clouds' (p. 65); as the Spanish ambulance speeds towards the hospital with Joy and Michael's body in the back, Joy sees only a blur of red and purple flowers pass by the vehicle's windows (p. 70); Joy articulates her sorrow at Michael's funeral in the form of a 'heart-shaped wreath covered in red carnations' (p. 118); whilst at Foresthouse the man in charge of the ward wears 'a lapel badge with TOM in red letters' (p. 123). Tellingly, as Joy begins the process of rehabilitation, the colour red becomes less prevalent. For example, as the patients are tasked with making Christmas cards 'Red's best but we've no red' (p. 219).

OOO

These regularly occurring typographical flourishes initially strike the reader as a way to denote the passing of time or a break in the linear narrative. To an extent, this is exactly the function that they do serve. Over the years, however, many critics have attempted to imbue these Os with much more symbolic resonance. Galloway herself has been quick to dismiss more fanciful critical interpretations – such as those which read the 'O' shapes as vaginas for example – by explaining how, at the time of writing the novel, she had given brief consideration to the idea that the shapes might indicate an exclamation of surprise or shock (as in the sound 'oh'). Despite Galloway's dismissal of tangential critical readings, there are some obvious ways in which these symbols can be read in the context of the story. As Joy remembers seeing Michael's dead body for the first time she notes: 'I look down and his mouth is a red O' (p. 40). The phrase 'red O' is repeated once more, followed by vacant space on the page. The space indicates time elapsing before 'OOO' brings the reader back to the present day. Furthermore, during her performance of normality for Dr Stead (p. 50), Joy acknowledges how her prescription pills are red in colour and circular in shape. It is an irony that the medication administered by the doctor to help Joy's recovery are the very things that remind Joy of the reason why she feels this way. We might also link the 'O' shapes to Joy's own mouth which is deprived of food throughout; to her own inarticulacy in the face of such intense grief. What is clear, however, is that the O shape is symbolic of Joy's anguish.

7. FURTHER READING

The novels

Foreign Parts (1994)

In her second novel, *Foreign Parts*, Galloway continues to explore aspects of female experience. If Joy Stone is the woman *in extremis* then Cassie Burns is a woman at the end of her tether. The novel is told from the point of view of Cassie as she enjoys – or perhaps endures – a holiday through northern France with her best friend, and fellow social worker, Rona. The objective of this holiday is not recreational, but rather familial obligation, as Rona sets out to locate her grandfather's grave in Normandy. Entirely planned and led by the organised Rona, this road trip through France is, for Cassie, a seeming inconvenience. Far from being the escapist holiday Cassie would like it to be, it is somewhat shambolic, never-ending, and tedious. The route chosen by Rona (through the sites of the battlefields in northern France) intentionally eschews the country's major cities – the bohemian and eclectic Paris, and the iconic Eiffel Tower at its heart, are only fleetingly glimpsed as the women skirt the city's periphery – in favour of small towns with which Rona feels some familial affinity, her grandfather having served there during the war. Rona certainly has ghosts to lay to rest on this holiday, but so, too, does Cassie, even if she is reluctant to admit it to her friend.

Cassie's acerbic observations serve as a glossary for the trip and provide a parodic counterpoint to the travel guide to France given to her by Rona and which she reads along the way. Utilising a technique similar to *The Trick is to Keep Breathing*, Galloway provides passages of text from the guidebook Cassie is reading, lending an authenticity to their experiences on one level, but revealing the disparity between fiction and fact on another. Each formal description of the French locale in the guidebook is sharply undercut by Cassie as she comments critically on the locals who inhabit the landscape, and the two Scottish foreigners who are passing through it.

Despite their continual movement through the French landscape, Rona's and Cassie's love lives are in stasis. Cassie's reflections on photographs that she has taken on previous holidays guide us through a series of holidays spent with old lovers, the mood of her reflections oscillating between sentimental and regretful nostalgia. Whilst Cassie seems hung up on ex-partners, she is curious as to why her friend has never seemed all that interested in having a partner:

> Rona?
> What?
> How come you don't bother with men much? I mean you never seem to miss not having one around.
>
> I feel the split second going ear to ear, tightening in my chest before I know it was ok to ask.
>
> Well there was Iain.
> I know there was Iain.
> [...]
> I suppose that was enough. I've just never wanted to repeat it badly enough. (p. 246)

Neither Cassie nor Rona is the woman *in extremis* as epitomised by the character of Joy Stone in *The Trick is to Keep Breathing*. Rather, they are women in limbo: middle-aged, directionless, partner-less. As their holiday – and bickering – wears on, neither woman is willing to concede defeat. By the end of the novel both women have confronted some form of personal truth about their unmarried status: why is Rona happy to be single, when Cassie seems to hinge all her hopes on men? Even if the women do not find their happily ever after on this trip to France, they do find some sort of contentment and comfort in each other's company.

Clara (2002)

On first appearances *Clara*, an intimate portrait of the life of Clara (Wieck) Schumann (1819–1896), seems unlike anything

Galloway has produced before or since. Yet first appearances are entirely deceptive. The further you delve into the novel, the more it seems wholly familiar, wholly 'Gallowayvian' in temperament. The novel charts the rise to musical prominence of Clara Wieck, a major cultural figure of German Romanticism, and casts imaginative light on the artistic influences underpinning the work of this pianist and composer. Sections one to four (pp. 11–189) outline the childhood and early teenage years of Clara as she undergoes an uncompromising regime of musical training at the hands of her overbearing father, Friedrich Wieck. At the novel's outset, Clara 'doesn't speak, has never spoken' (p. 13), people believe her to be either 'poor or simple; others that she's both' (p. 13). Despite her inarticulacy, Herr Wieck, an accomplished piano teacher, and a man desperate to mould at least one of his children into 'the greatest pianist he could fashion, his brightness, a star' (p. 23), sees something profoundly promising in his youngest child. Herr Wieck's punishing programme of training transforms Clara from a shy girl into a child prodigy with the popular appeal to sell out concert halls in some of Europe's finest cities, and with the talent to obtain the honour of 'Court Virtuosa in Ordinary to the Emperor of Austria'.

As Clara's prodigious talents become apparent, Herr Wieck's 'little *Clärchen*' becomes his obsession. The thought of her being attracted to the opposite sex, of entering into relationships with men, fills Friedrich with vehement anger, for in this carnal desire 'she is like any other woman' (p. 159). According to Wieck, she will allow her passions to come between her and her art. Wieck's refusal to acknowledge Clara's transformation from a child into a young woman forces a distance between father and daughter and drives Clara straight into the arms of the man she will eventually marry. It is this intense romance which drives the middle sections of the novel.

As well as the musical transformation, this novel charts the personal transformation of Clara Wieck into Mrs Robert Schumann, a transition spanning ten years from when Clara met Robert at the age of nine. The course of true love never did run smooth, and Clara must take her father to court in order to be allowed to marry Schumann. Galloway depicts the enduring relationship between Clara and a man eight years her senior with an astonishing lyricism and intensity, facilitated by her adroit use of layout and structure. *Clara* is, arguably, Galloway's most innovative and typographically sophisticated novel; the narrative of Clara's and Robert's love affair is told through fragmented discourse, epistolary correspondence, lists and diary extracts. The most beautiful additions to the novel are, perhaps, the pages watermarked with musical scores, often music composed by Robert for Clara.

Like *The Trick*, *Clara* is also a novel thematically underpinned by the concept of dependency. Whilst it is the female figure in the *Trick* who cannot depend on anyone – not least herself – we find the opposite to be the case in *Clara*. Both Friedrich Wieck and Robert Schumann are helplessly reliant on Clara for their continued success or balanced state of mind. As the novel progresses we understand that the novel hinges on the theme of thraldom. Both Clara and Robert are enthralled by each other – Robert is unable to be without his Clara, and Clara unable to leave her ill husband, whilst Herr Wick's attempts to enslave the child Clara to her piano are echoed later when he attempts to prohibit Clara from marrying. Each character in turn is a slave to their art. A comparative reading of *Clara* and Galloway's seminal novel, *The Trick*, would certainly be a worthwhile exercise.

Short fiction

Blood (1991)
On the back of her success with her debut novel, Galloway's *Blood*, a collection of twenty-two short stories, was warmly received. The dazzling generic, linguistic, stylistic and thematic diversity of the works contained in this collection provides an excellent showcase for Galloway's mastery of the short story form.

The title story from the collection opens with a graphic portrayal of a female's visit to the dentist. Both characters in the opening sequence are anonymous. The man's identity is further obscured by the fact that his face is concealed behind his surgical mask. Galloway's treatment turns a somewhat commonplace procedure into an event with threatening and violent undertones. The 'bones in [the dentist's] hand were bruising her lip' (p. 1), and he must slacken 'the grip' on his pliers 'momentarily, catching his breath' (p. 1) before re-applying the pressure. Galloway's vivid description of the extraction is connotative of childbirth: 'her spine lifting, arching from the seat [...] he was holding something up in the metal clamp; great bloody lump of it' (p. 1). The connection between the extraction and pregnancy is solidified when the female protagonist is handed a sanitary towel with which to stem the flow of blood: 'Something slithered in her stomach [...] then a twinge in her back, a recognisable contraction' (p. 6). The narrator admits that it was 'hard to accept her body had grown this thing' (p. 7). On return to school, the persona experiences the cramping and swelling indicative of the onset of menstruation. The irony of having a sanitary towel for the blood in her mouth, but not one for her menstrual blood is not lost on the reader or on the character. Having prepared a makeshift pad, the persona makes her way to the sanctuary of the music room. The story has yet one more horrific scene for us. The male music student returns and mistakenly identifies the piece of Mozart the girl is playing as Haydn. Eager to correct him, the girl forgets the tide of blood swirling around her mouth. The blood spills 'over the white keys' and drips 'onto the clean tile floor' (p. 8). Just as in *The Trick*, 'Blood' sees Galloway explore aspects of the female condition. With the nameless female rendered voiceless by the dentist's brutality, we have a character who cannot articulate her experience. Nor can she challenge the male 'authority' in the form of both the dentist and the music student.

Blood also showcases more experimental 'episodes' – or vignettes – signposted by the shared title 'Scenes from the Life [...]'. Numbering four in total, the 'Scenes from the Life' begin, unconventionally, at 'No. 23'. The sequence does not run sequentially from 23 to 27. We find: 'Scenes from the Life No. 23: Paternal Advice'; 'Scenes from the Life No. 26: The

Community and the Senior Citizen'; 'Scenes from the Life No. 24: Bikers'; and 'Scenes from the Life No. 27: Living In'. When asked in interview about the naming process for this partially complete arrangement of 'scenes', Galloway explained how it arose from necessity (writers, after all, have to call their pieces something). Whilst the numbering system might be arbitrary, there is nothing accidental about the use of the word 'scenes', which is hugely evocative of the theatrical. In 'Scenes from the Life No. 23: Paternal Advice', for example, we are supposed to identify aspects of a dramatic script such as stage directions: 'SAMMY exhales noisily. He appears to be mulling over some tricky problem [...] we are in the thick of it' (p. 11).

As well as exhibiting Galloway's stylistic experimentation, this particular 'scene' showcases Galloway's sardonic wit. With her portrayal of the tough-loving father, Sammy, eager to impart pearls of wisdom to his son, Galloway simultaneously taps into and parodies the rich contemporary vein of Scottish literature in which the experience of the archetypal West of Scotland working-class male is presented and explored. The relative sentimentality of the opening pages of the story – in which Sammy toils anxiously to find the right words with which to teach his son a valuable life lesson – is comically subverted by the story's *moralitas*. Having lifted Wee Sammy onto the mantelpiece, Sammy gently cajoles his son to jump off into his arms. The son duly agrees, assured in the knowledge that his trustworthy father will catch him. As Wee Sammy begins his descent, Sammy sidesteps, and the child plummets to the floor. Sammy finally finds the right words with which to deliver an unexpected truism to his son; in his rich Glasgow demotic Sammy calmly asserts: 'Let that be a lesson to you son. Trust nae cunt' (p. 16). The seemingly cruel ending to Wee Sammy's lesson belies the warm humanity of the piece.

Like 'No. 23', 'Scenes from the Life No. 26: The Community and the Senior Citizen' opens and closes with extended passages of prose rendered like stage directions. Sandwiched in the middle is a stilted dialogue between a HEALTH VISITOR and an OLD WOMAN; this particular scene, between an

uncommunicative patient and an unaware healthcare professional, has the feeling of a preparatory sketch for Joy Stone's
meeting with the Health Visitor in *The Trick is to Keep
Breathing* (pp. 20–24). There are significant overlaps in the
characters of Joy and the old woman, given that both struggle
with the articulation of their thoughts, are isolated in their
community and attempt to take their own life. The ritual of
taking tea is performed in both texts for the benefit of the
visiting nurse, and notably both women are keen to eradicate
the evidence of the meeting with the Health Visitor having
ever taken place. Where Joy 'rub[s] out the creases on the
chair where [they] have been sitting' (p. 24), the old woman:

> [...] begins by clearing the tea-things and carrying them off
> to the room on the right [...] with a jerky delicacy that suggests
> distaste, rinses the cups, saucers and single spoon at the cold
> tap [...] the milk carton is waiting. She takes it from the tray
> and tips the last of it down the sink, erasing white stains
> with swirling water. (p. 52)

As 'Scenes from the Life No. 26' progresses, the role of the
reader shifts from the interested spectator to the prying voyeur,
as an interlude (signalled by italics) provides us an insight
into the private life of the old woman beyond the façade of
that morning's visitation. In this interlude the old woman is
seen alone and vulnerable, vomiting in her bedroom. The stage
directions are interrupted by a thought from the narrator –
'perhaps we should go' (p. 53).

The direct address of the reader through the pronoun 'we'
implicates the reader. When we think the old woman is isolated
we may feel guilt, but we are quickly exonerated: 'this is a
sheltered house [...] Ah. A little weight drops from our necks'
(p. 54). Only towards the end of the short story is the 'old
woman' given her full married title. We note that Galloway
opts not to reveal the character's first name. She is defined by
her marital status. The final 'performance' in this scene is a
carefully executed suicide bid. In a cold conclusion to the short
story, the narrator cuts from the scene. There is a sense of

inevitability about what happens next. Unlike the vomiting scene, we are not allowed to see (nor indeed might we want to view) the final minutes of the old woman's life. Her death, as seemingly her life, is irrelevant to us. The narrator withdraws from the scene asserting: 'Let her wait on. We have other things to do'. In this 'Scene from the Life' Galloway powerfully renders the experience of isolation and exclusion, admiring the grim determination in the characters portrayed. Galloway is fierce in her critique of society's indifference towards the socially excluded, the weak and the vulnerable. In Galloway's fiction the narrative perspective is almost always that of the female, but what is striking in this particular story is the 'old' age of the female protagonist.

In 'David', Galloway explores the shadowy beginnings of an illicit relationship between a teacher and a pupil; the eponymous David appearing as a more developed character in *The Trick is to Keep Breathing*. Told from the point of view of the female, this short story is a candid admission of the part she played in instigating a sexual relationship with a school-aged pupil. Overstepping professional boundaries as a teacher, the anonymous protagonist of this short story and her teaching colleague, Carol, venture into 'uncharted territory' (p. 36) by attending a house party hosted by a pupil called Sam from the school at which they both teach. There are details of that first evening together that the narrator claims not to fully recollect. Whether as a result of the alcohol consumed at the party, whether as a result of time, or whether as a result of her being unwilling to remember, this account is unreliable. Despite her hazy memory, the narrator recounts with vivid clarity their first sexual encounter:

> Our teeth touched, mouths open. I felt him swallow, the skin on my lip stretch till it split, a sudden give from the tightness and I was sliding my hands, tugging on the thin shirt. (p. 38)

The effect of this short story is to allow the reader familiar with *The Trick* to further contemplate one of the more throw-

away, but also fairly sinister, admissions from Joy Stone in
the novel that she instigated the affair. For those unfamiliar
with the novel, we may appreciate Galloway's treatment of
such a taboo subject – the abuse of position. The short story
ends with the repetition of the phrase 'What else to say?'. With
the confession complete, the reader is left to make the ultimate
judgement.

Where You Find It (1997)
In *Where You Find It,* her second collection of short stories,
Galloway turns to the subject of love, in all its complex forms.
The clichéd front cover – garish pink satin, roses and sandwich
love-hearts – belies Galloway's fresh treatment of an age-old
concern. The relationships presented in this collection are
often well worn-in – sometimes even worn-out – as Galloway
explores the intricacies and strains of pre- and post-marital
modern relationships.

The short story 'Bisex' takes the form of an imagined scenario,
in which an anonymous narrator speculates about their
partner's fidelity. The gender of the narrator is ambiguous,
but it becomes clear that the subject of the speculation is a
male partner. The narrator imagines their partner meeting
a man in the pub ('I don't know how you begin with these men',
p. 89), before graphically envisaging him making love to the
stranger. The narrator comes to realise that their relationship
is not serving either of them well:

> I do not want you to be alone. And I know somewhere deeper
> that's all you want too. What I imagine is nothing as real as
> that longing, as what you're really looking for. The thing
> that is not, will never be me. (p. 90)

In 'Peeping Tom' we find a female narrator equally disaf-
fected with her relationship with an inattentive partner, Roddy.
As Moira reveals more details of their relationship, the suggestion that Roddy is having an affair (an affair to which the
narrator is oblivious) crystallises. The initial sexual excitement
('used to be as soon as I heard running water, I'd start shedding